Introducti

Betws-y-Coed, the popular gateway into
amidst a beautiful landscape of wooded r
containing numerous hidden lakes. After Th
over the Conwy opened in 1815, the hither
important staging post on the London to Holyhead Irish Mail coach road.
During the 19thC the stunning scenery attracted many eminent travellers, visitors and artists to this part of North Wales, by road, by river as far as Trefriw,
then an important inland port, and later by railway.

The area around Betws-y-Coed and the upland edges of the Conwy valley, lying within Snowdonia National Park's eastern edge, is delightful walking country, where you can quickly leave the crowds behind. The 24 circular
walks in this book explore its diverse landscape and history. There are walks
by rivers, past waterfalls, including the famous Swallow Falls, over hills and
up Tal y Fan mountain. They follow miners' paths and waymarked trails
through Gwydwr Forest Park past upland lakes and the relics of a once thriving lead-mining industry. They take you along Roman roads, and past ancient
upland burial chambers, standing stones and remote churches.

The routes, which range from a ¾ mile visit to the famous Fairy Glen to
a challenging 10 mile walk to remote lakes set beneath the Carneddau mountain range, follow public rights of way or permissive paths and are within the
capability of most people. *A key feature is that most individual routes, as well
as containing shorter walk options, can easily be linked with others, to provide
longer day walks, if required.* This increases choice and encourages creativity
in your walking routes. Walking boots are recommended, along with appropri-
ate clothing to protect against the elements. Many of the walks are accessible
by regular bus service 19 (Traveline 0870 608 2 608) or the Conwy Valley
Railway (08457 484950).

Each walk has a detailed map and description which enables the route to
be followed without difficulty. Bear in mind though that changes in detail can
occur at any time. The location of each walk is shown on the back cover and a
summary of their key features is also given. This includes an estimated walking time, but allow more time to enjoy the scenery and sights.

Remember that the condition of paths can vary according to season and
weather. Refer any problems encountered to Conwy Highways Department
(01492 575440). Please observe the country code.

The *Conwy Valley Rail Initiative*, which is a partnership of community
stakeholders supporting the Conwy Valley Branch Line from Llandudno to
Blaenau Ffestiniog, is pleased to be associated with this excellent publication,
which will be invaluable for visitors and locals alike who enjoy the spendour
and the outdoor wonders of the Conwy and Lledr Valleys.

Enjoy your walking!

MINERS BRIDGE

DESCRIPTION A popular 1¾ mile riverside walk following the Afon Llugwy to the Miners Bridge, a favourite subject for generations of artists, returning by a quiet attractive country road. Allow about 1 hour.

START Pont-y-Pair, Betws-y-Coed [SH 792567]

DIRECTIONS This ancient stone bridge lies just off the A5 in the centre of Betws-y-Coed.

*P*ont-y-Pair (Bridge of the Cauldron) is said to have been built across the Afon Llugwy during the 15thC by a mason called Howel, who died before its completion. Further upstream is the unusual inclined Miners Bridge, described in an 1890 book as 'a sort of ladder with rails spanning a roaring torrent', which enabled miners from Pentre Du and Rhiwddolion to get to Gwydyr's lead-mines, which were a major source of employment during the 19thC. It stands near the crossing place of the Sarn Helen Roman road.

I At the far side of the bridge turn LEFT on a minor road past a car park/toilets. Just beyond, join the signposted riverside path and follow it through the edge of the wood to cross a ladder-stile. Continue with the riverside path along the edge of a large field, over a footbridge and on to cross a ladder-stile at the far end. A short section of wooded riverside path brings you to the Miners Bridge. Here, turn RIGHT to follow the signposted path angling up through the conifers to the road. Turn RIGHT and follow this quiet country road back to Pont-y-Pair.

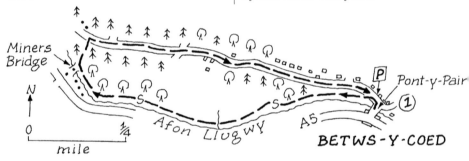

WALK 2

LLYN ELSI AND SARN HELEN

DESCRIPTION A 4½ mile walk up to the attractive upland lake of Llyn Elsi, lying hidden from sight on a forested spur above the town, offering extensive views. It features a section of the Sarn Helen Roman Road, which ran from Caerhun in the Conwy Valley to Carmarthen,

the Miners Bridge and a riverside return. Allow about 2 1/2 hours. There is a shorter walk option missing out Llyn Elsi.

START Pont-y-Pair, Betws-y-Coed [SH 792567] See **Walk 1**.

I From the bridge follow the main road (A5) west out of Betws-y-Coed. After nearly ½ mile, take the signposted path along the lane to Hendre Farm campsite. Cross a stile at the camping field entrance and go up

an old green track, soon enclosed by walls, to cross a ladder-stile into a wood. Follow the path rising steadily up through the trees, later passing a stile, to reach the bend of a forestry track. Cross a stile by a gate on the right and

2

go up a stony path. After about 150 yards you pass an old tramway on your right near a ruined building. Continue ahead up the path, soon bending

Miners Bridge   A5

Sarn Helen

0 ——— ¼ mile

N

walk 3

quarry

monument

Llyn Elsi

Pont-y-Pair

① **BETWS-Y-COED**

the barn to go through a kissing gate. Follow the waymarked path up and across a small grassy ridge – *offering good mountain views* – soon passing to the right of a small reedy area, before gradually bearing LEFT, then half-RIGHT down to a wide path by the edge of a forest. Turn RIGHT and follow the path leading away from the forest to join a stony track. (The next section to the A5 follows the former Sarn Helen Roman road.)

4 Continue ahead past a ruin and on down past a farmhouse. Follow the lane to a forestry road. Go through the gate opposite and one just below, and follow the delightful enclosed stony path down past Canol-yr-allt and over a cross-track. Shortly, cross a footbridge, then a stile and continue down the track to join a lane leading to the A5. Follow the signposted path opposite to cross the Miners Bridge. Turn RIGHT and follow the riverside path back to Pont-y-Pair.

LEFT past the former 19th C Hafod-las slate quarry to cross a ladder-stile. Continue up through an old gateway and on up to cross a stile by a barn. Turn RIGHT and follow a waymarked path up an old track to eventually reach another green track. (For the shorter walk, turn right to reach an access track by Hafod Las. Follow it left, crossing a ladder-stile, to turn right along a forestry track to point **3**.)

2 For Llyn Elsi, turn LEFT and follow the waymarked path, over a ladder-stile, and on up near a wall to a forestry track. Continue with the path opposite to reach a stony path. Follow it LEFT up to the monument above Llyn Elsi. *It was erected to commemorate the opening of the Betws-y-Coed waterworks in 1914, when the lake became a reservoir providing water for the town. Good views of Moel Siabod and the Carneddau mountains.* Return down the stony path and follow it past your outward path, soon descending to bear RIGHT just before a footbridge near the dam to reach a forestry track. Follow it LEFT for 1/3 mile.

3 Shortly after leaving the forest, turn LEFT through a gate and go along an access track towards Pant yr hyddod, then follow the signposted diverted footpath to pass behind

Miners Bridge

3

LLYN ELSI

DESCRIPTION A 6 mile walk (**A**) exploring the attractive part-wooded upland area above Betws-y-Coed containing the attractive hidden lake of Llyn Elsi. The route follows a waymarked forest trail up to Llyn Elsi, then completes a circuit of the lake. After enjoying extensive views from the commemorative monument, the route meanders down through old quarry workings and woodland to cross the Miners Bridge for a delightful riverside return. Allow about 3½ hours. The route can be shortened to a 4¾ mile walk (**B**) by going direct to the monument.
START Car park by toilets, near the railway station, Betws-y-Coed [SH 795565] – both signposted from the main A5 road.

I Follow a pathway past the toilets to cross the main road. Turn RIGHT past the PO/stores, then LEFT up a road, soon bearing RIGHT beneath Church Hill and above St. Mary's church. Shortly, take a signposted Llyn Elsi path on the left up past the side of Gwalia to enter a wood. Now follow a stony track rising steadily through the trees, marked by blue/white-topped posts, past side paths to eventually pass an open area giving views across the wooded valley. When the track splits take the RIGHT fork, marked by white-topped posts, which mark the trail to Llyn Elsi. At a track junction keep ahead. At the next junction, go up the LEFT fork. Keep ahead at the next junction, then turn LEFT at the following one to reach Llyn Elsi. (For **Walk B**, on the bend, take a path leading direct to the monument above the lake.)

2 The main walk now follows the track along the eastern side of the lake. Just beyond the end of the lake the track descends. Shortly, go up a stony path on the right marked by a white-topped post, and follow the clear trail path, with occasional glimpses of the lake, along its western side. Just beyond a white-topped post on a bend overlooking a narrow arm of the lake, take a path on the right down to cross a footbridge and follow it near the water's edge to reach

a prominent viewpoint across the lake. The path now meanders round the side of the lake to the dam, goes up steps, then crosses a footbridge to reach a path junction below the dam. Follow the path ahead up to the monument. *It was erected to commemorate the opening of the Betws-y-Coed waterworks in 1914, when the lake became a reservoir providing water for the town.* There are good views from Moel Siabod to the Carneddau mountains. Return down the path.

3 At the bottom of the slope, take a path on the right through an area of bracken and rowen to cross a forestry track. Go down a path almost opposite, soon alongside a wall, to cross a ladder-stile. Continue down the waymarked path and about 70 yards before a stone barn ahead, swing sharp RIGHT to follow another waymarked path along a green track down to a barn. Cross a stile and turn LEFT down the path, through an old gateway and over a ladder-stile. Continue down path past the edge of the former 19thC Hafod-las slate quarry, soon bending RIGHT. After about 100 yards, near an old quarry building, turn LEFT along a former tramway.

4 At a gate, descend a path to cross a stream leading from a mine adit, and continue between a spoil heap and two quarry buildings. Just beyond the second building, the path descends to cross a stile on the left. Continue up the edge of the field beneath spoil heaps to cross a stile into a wood. Follow the path through the trees, briefly joining a stream, to reach a track. Follow it LEFT. At a track junction, keep ahead down the track to cross a stream. About 150 yards further, at a large boulder, and just before the bend ahead, turn RIGHT down a path towards the nearby small waterfall, then down through the trees to a minor road. Follow it RIGHT past houses to the A5. Follow the signposted path opposite to cross the Miners Bridge – *just as miners would have done on their way to work in the lead-mines during the 19thC.*

5 Turn RIGHT alongside the fence and follow the riverside path along the edge of a wood, long field, then another wood, to

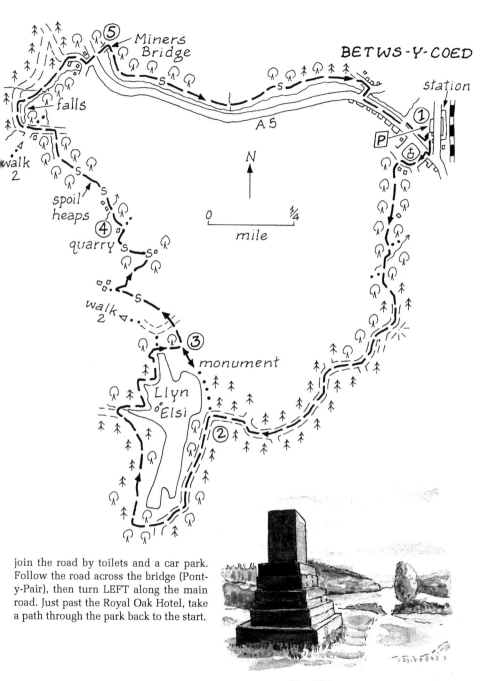

BETWS-Y-COED

station

Miners Bridge

falls

walk 2

spoil heaps

quarry

walk 2

monument

Llyn Elsi

A5

N

0 ¼

mile

join the road by toilets and a car park. Follow the road across the bridge (Pont-y-Pair), then turn LEFT along the main road. Just past the Royal Oak Hotel, take a path through the park back to the start.

Llyn Elsi monument

LLUGWY AND LLEDR VALLEYS

DESCRIPTION An 8 mile walk linking the beautiful wooded Llugwy and Lledr valleys. The route follows the riverside path to the Miners Bridge, then takes Sarn Helen, the former Roman road to Mid-Wales, up across the part-wooded hillside, reaching a height of about 800 feet, before descending into the Lledr valley. Further delightful riverside walking is followed by a climb up the initially steep wooded slopes to Llyn Elsi for a final descent through the forest. Allow about 5 hours. The route can be undertaken as two linear walks from Pont-y-Pant halt – a request stop on the Betws-y-Coed – Blaenau Ffestiniog railway line: a 4 mile return via Sarn Helen, or a 4½ mile return via Llyn Elsi following the route from point **3**.

START Car park/toilets near the Railway Station, Betws-y-Coed [SH 795565] – both signposted from the main A5 road.

I Take the pathway angling away from the toilets to join the main road by the Royal Oak Hotel. Follow the road to cross the bridge (Pont-y-Pair) over the river, then turn LEFT. Just past the toilets, join the riverside path, which you follow for ¾ mile to cross the inclined Miners Bridge. Go up steps and follow the path ahead to the A5. Go along the lane opposite. After passing Bryn Tirion, follow a track ahead through a gate and up to a stile. Continue up the stony path, over a footbridge, and on up to a track junction. Keep ahead and follow the delightful enclosed stony path up to reach a forestry track via two gates. Go up the lane opposite and through a gate just beyond a farmhouse. Continue up the track.

2 Just beyond a small ruin, follow the stony track down and on through a gate by a stream. Continue up the track past ruined houses of Rhiwddolion – *a once thriving community that was abandoned during the early 20thC following the closure of local mines and quarries*. Go through a gate and follow the track, soon across an open area of cleared forest and young trees, over a forestry track, and on to cross a ladder-stile at the forest perimeter. Follow the track across open country, later descending to join a lane. Follow it down. After a house, cross a stile on the left. Follow the path to the A470. Take the road opposite over the river Lledr beneath Plas Hall Hotel.

3 At the junction, turn LEFT to pass behind the hotel. At the entrance to the Outdoor Education Centre, continue ahead down the enclosed path, across the driveway, through a gate and across a stream. The path now runs beneath the railway line, then briefly joins the river, before continuing alongside a wall. It then runs close to both the railway and the river to go through a small metal gate, then a waymarked wooden one. Turn LEFT to follow the wooded riverside path passing above a gorge. At the wood end cross a ladder-stile, and follow the riverside path to Tan Aeldroch farm. Turn LEFT down its access track to cross a stile on the right. Follow the track through the riverside campsite and the next field to cross a stile. Follow the main path up to join the railway. Pass under the railway arch and follow the path alongside the fence on your right round to cottages.

4 Here do a U-turn to pass behind the first cottage and on down the walled track to its bend. Go through the old gateway ahead and follow the path to cross a footbridge over the river, then through the trees to the A470. Cross the road and follow it with care under nearby Pont Gethin – *the railway viaduct built in 1875-78 by Gethin, a local builder* – then turn RIGHT along the track leading to Craig Lledr. Shortly, take a signposted path. It angles through the trees, crosses a footbridge, then rises steeply up the wooded hillside near the stream, later becoming less

6

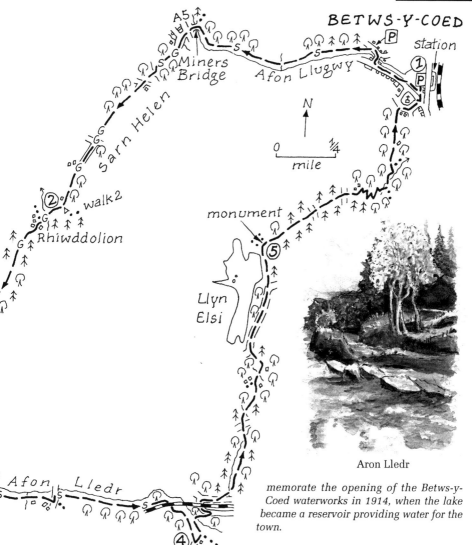

BETWS-Y-COED

station

Miners Bridge

Afon Llugwy

A5

Sarn Helen

N

0   ¼ mile

monument

② walk 2

Rhiwddolion

⑤

Llyn Elsi

Afon Lledr

④

Aron Lledr

memorate the opening of the Betws-y-Coed waterworks in 1914, when the lake became a reservoir providing water for the town.

steep and crossing the stream. At a forestry track, take the path opposite. After a small ruin, it rises to join another path coming in on the left from another ruin. Cross a stream and follow the path past a ruin glimpsed to your right, then briefly alongside a wall, to soon emerge on a forestry track by Llyn Elsi. Follow it RIGHT along the lake's eastern side. On the bend continue ahead on a path up to the monument. *It was erected to com-*

5 Looking north, take a path leading RIGHT, shortly entering the forest, later descending to cross a forestry track. Continue through the forest, over another track, and down a stony path in a part-open section to pass ruins. The path now zig-zags down the wooded slope, then crosses a footbridge to reach a track. Follow it down through the forest to reach the road behind St. Mary's church. Follow it RIGHT down to the main road and back to the start.

FAIRY GLEN

DESCRIPTION A choice of short walks, easily combined, near the famous Fairy Glen, a deep narrow wooded river gorge, popular since Victorian times. **Walk A** follows a delightful ¾ mile privately owned circular trail to the Fairy Glen, with a nominal charge payable. **Walk B** is an enjoyable there and back 1½ mile popular Victorian stroll towards Conwy Falls along the former London to Holyhead tollgate road, superseded by Telford's new road (A5) in the early 19thC, and now a track/path. Continuing to the entrance to Conwy Falls nowadays involves walking on the busy A5, with no pavement and tight bend, and is not recommended!

START Fairy Glen car park [SH 799546]

DIRECTIONS Just south of Waterloo Bridge, Betws-y-Coed, take the A470 towards Dolgellau/Dolwyddelan. Immediately after Fairy Glen Hotel and just before Beaver Bridge turn left up a track signposted Fairy Glen/car park/Cymanog Isaf Farm to a car park (small charge payable).

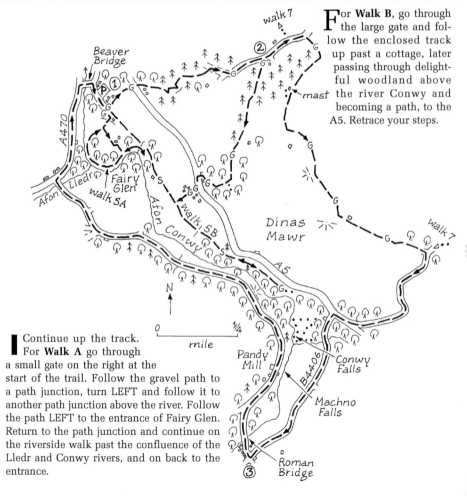

For **Walk B**, go through the large gate and follow the enclosed track up past a cottage, later passing through delightful woodland above the river Conwy and becoming a path, to the A5. Retrace your steps.

Continue up the track. For **Walk A** go through a small gate on the right at the start of the trail. Follow the gravel path to a path junction, turn LEFT and follow it to another path junction above the river. Follow the path LEFT to the entrance of Fairy Glen. Return to the path junction and continue on the riverside walk past the confluence of the Lledr and Conwy rivers, and on back to the entrance.

WALK 6

DINAS MAWR, CONWY AND MACHNO FALLS

DESCRIPTION A varied 5 mile walk (**A**) which combines well with the Fairy Glen trail. The route rises from the Conwy Valley, initially through woodland, to follow a delightful old track across attractive upland country adjoining the dominant crag of Dinas Mawr, offering extensive views. After descending to the valley, with the option of visiting Conwy falls (small charge), it then follows a scenic quiet country road past an ancient packhorse bridge, Machno falls and the Conwy gorge. Allow about 3 hours. An alternative 2 mile walk (**B**) is described.

START As **Walk 5** or on the minor road near Beaver Bridge [SH 798547]

I Continue up the track and go through a bridle gate opposite the Fairy Glen trail entrance. Follow the path up past the house to the A5. Cross the road with care to go through a gap in the wall opposite. Follow a path rising steadily along the wood edge beside a wall. It then bends LEFT to zig-zag up the wooded slope and on more directly to join a wall. The gradient now eases as the path follows the wall up to a forestry track. Turn RIGHT to soon join a road. Go through a gate and continue up the road.

2 For **Walk B**, at a wood corner, go through a kissing gate on the right. Follow the path alongside the wall, over a stream, soon alongside another wall, and down to a kissing gate. The path descends the birch-covered slopes leading to Dinas Mawr, briefly more steeply past a telegraph post then a path on the left, before easing to go through a kissing gate, and on to reach the A5 – caution! Cross the road and turn LEFT to take a signposted path through a gate. At old buildings, bend RIGHT through a gate. Go down past the first of other old buildings, through a gateway and down the field to an enclosed green track. Follow it RIGHT past a cottage back to the start.
For **Walk A** follow the road past a cottage and at a gate across the road, turn RIGHT up alongside a wall to go through a gate at the wood corner. Follow the path alongside the wall boundary of the wood, past a radio transmitter mast to join a green track, which you follow for ¾ mile across scenic upland pasture past Dinas Mawr to a minor road. Follow it down to the A5. Cross the road with care to reach the nearby junction. Turn LEFT on the B4406 towards Penmachno. Nearby is the Conwy Falls Café/Restaurant, from where paths run to the waterfalls. Follow the road across the Conwy gorge and on for about ½ mile.

3 At a cross-roads by a former chapel and cottages, turn RIGHT to pass the former Penmachno Woollen Mill – *built originally in the 1830s as a fulling mill powered by water from the adjoining Afon Machno. Just downstream is the packhorse bridge, known as 'Roman Bridge'.* Follow the road to Pandy Mill, opposite which a path leads past the ruined corn mill to Machno Falls. Continue along the road, past a viewpoint of the Conwy gorge and later with Dinas Mawr towering above the valley. *Dinas Mawr greatly impressed George Borrow, which he described as 'an immense mountain' in his famous book 'Wild Wales', when he walked beneath it in 1854.* Eventually, the road descends to cross the 15thC Pont-ar-Lledr to reach the A470. Cross the road and follow a walkway/cycleway RIGHT to Beaver Bridge. Cross the bridge and return to the start.

MYNYDD GARTHMYN AND CAPEL GARMON BURIAL CHAMBER

DESCRIPTION A 6½ mile (**A**) walk exploring the attractive upland area to the east of Betws-y-Coed, featuring a classic viewpoint overlooking the town and the Conwy valley from Mynydd Garthmyn (823 feet), the old droving village of Capel Garmon, and an impressive Neolithic burial chamber. Allow about 4 hours. The route offers an alternative 4½ mile walk

(**B**), and a 2¾ mile walk (**C**), missing out the burial chamber. This walk can easily be accessed from Betws-y-Coed via **Walk 8**.

START Lay-by on A470 near Waterloo Bridge [SH 799560].

DIRECTIONS After leaving Betws-y-Coed via Waterloo Bridge, turn left on the A470 towards Llanwrst to park in the second lay-by on the left.

1 Continue along the roadside pathway, then take the road signposted to Capel Garmon. Follow it up the hillside, later passing a house and signposted path on the right. Just past a row of terraced cottages at a telephone box, take a signposted path through a kissing gate on the left. Continue ahead up steps and past Garmonfa to join a track. Follow it LEFT to cross a ladder-stile at the entrance to Pen-y-Foel. Follow its access track for about 20 yards, then take a way-marked path on the right. It meanders up through an area of birch, rowan, bracken, heather and gorse – *soon with good views of Moel Siabod, the Glyders, Tryfan and the Carneddau Mountains.*

2 After crossing a stile, head half-LEFT for about 25 yards, then go up the slope between bracken before bearing half-LEFT to follow a path contouring below a small rocky ridge on your right to reach a small pool. Go up on the nearby crag to a superb viewpoint. Return to the pool, and just beyond, bear LEFT to work your way up onto the impressive rocky summit of Mynydd Garthmyn. Looking south, descend half-RIGHT, passing to the left of trees to join your outward path back to the stile. Return to the road and turn LEFT. (For **Walk C** turn right down the road, then take the signposted path on the left. Cross over the stream and take the right fork of the track to rejoin the main route at point **6**.)

3 Just past Garthmyn, go through a kissing gate on the right. Go across the field and through gates into the next field, then bear LEFT to go through a kissing gate. Go across the field and through another kissing gate to a track. *Capel Garmon with its church is prominent ahead.* Go through a small gate opposite and continue ahead across the reedy field to a kissing gate just beyond a clump of trees. Head up towards buildings and on past the front of a stone cottage. At its boundary wall corner, turn LEFT up to go through the field corner. Turn RIGHT, then angle away from the fence up to the churchyard wall. Follow it LEFT to reach the road opposite the school via a kissing gate. *The village stands on an old drovers' route along which sheep and cattle once passed on their way to market at Llanrwst or further afield in England.* Turn RIGHT. Follow the road through the village past the 19thC church and the White Horse Inn to a junction by a chapel. (For **Walk B** turn right and follow the road to rejoin the main walk at point **5**.)

4 Follow the road ahead out of the village, past two signposted paths on the right, As the road begins to rise cross a ladder-stile on the right. Follow the boundary on your left round to a kissing gate and continue with the path to Tyn-y-Coed farm. Go through the farmyard and up its access lane. On the bend turn RIGHT down to go through a small gate. Go along the field edge, and midway, go through a gate in the boundary. Head half-LEFT to reach the burial chamber. Cross a stile just beyond. After 50 yards the waymarked path crosses a small rocky knoll to go through a kissing gate. Go up through

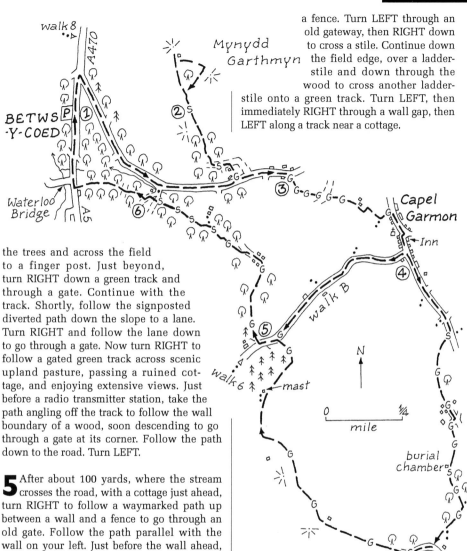

a fence. Turn LEFT through an old gateway, then RIGHT down to cross a stile. Continue down the field edge, over a ladder-stile and down through the wood to cross another ladder-stile onto a green track. Turn LEFT, then immediately RIGHT through a wall gap, then LEFT along a track near a cottage.

the trees and across the field to a finger post. Just beyond, turn RIGHT down a green track and through a gate. Continue with the track. Shortly, follow the signposted diverted path down the slope to a lane. Turn RIGHT and follow the lane down to go through a gate. Now turn RIGHT to follow a gated green track across scenic upland pasture, passing a ruined cottage, and enjoying extensive views. Just before a radio transmitter station, take the path angling off the track to follow the wall boundary of a wood, soon descending to go through a gate at its corner. Follow the path down to the road. Turn LEFT.

5 After about 100 yards, where the stream crosses the road, with a cottage just ahead, turn RIGHT to follow a waymarked path up between a wall and a fence to go through an old gate. Follow the path parallel with the wall on your left. Just before the wall ahead, the path bears RIGHT, soon alongside it, then briefly descends past a small tree encrusted crag to go through a small gate at the end of a stone barn. Follow the waymarked path through the boarding kennels/cattery and continue up its access lane. Shortly, go half-LEFT on a waymarked path, soon descending to a kissing gate. Continue ahead down the field. At a post, go half-LEFT to another post. Just beyond, bear RIGHT to cross a stile above a gate. Descend half-LEFT guided by posts to

6 On the bend, take a signposted path on the right. Follow it down alongside a wall through the trees, over a track, and on down to suddenly emerge on the A5 alongside the Ty Gwyn Hotel (caution). Cross the road. Turn RIGHT back to the start.

11

WALK 8
ST. MICHAEL'S CHURCH

DESCRIPTION A 2¾ mile (**A**) or 1½ mile (**B**) walk exploring the fine riverside scenery at Betws-y-Coed and featuring the 14thC St. Michael's church, which served as the parish church until the larger St.Mary's was built to accommodate the religious needs of 19thC tourists. The route follows the Afon Llugwy to its confluence with the Afon Conwy, which it then accompanies to the church. Walk A crosses the river by a delightful suspension bridge and follows a path to the road for a return across the attractive cast-iron Waterloo Bridge built in 1815 by Thomas Telford to carry the London-Holyhead road. Allow about 1½ hours. Both finish with an optional visit to the Railway Museum.

START Car park near the Railway Station, Betws-y-Coed. [SH 795565] – both signposted from the main A5 road.

bridge constructed by the Royal Engineers in WW1 as a replacement for stepping stones just downstream. Follow the enclosed path to a farm and up its driveway to the road. Turn RIGHT and follow the roadside pathway to the junction. Turn RIGHT over Waterloo Bridge. Follow the road into Betws-y-Coed, then take the road on the right across the railway line to pass St. Michael's church to reach the Railway Museum and station.

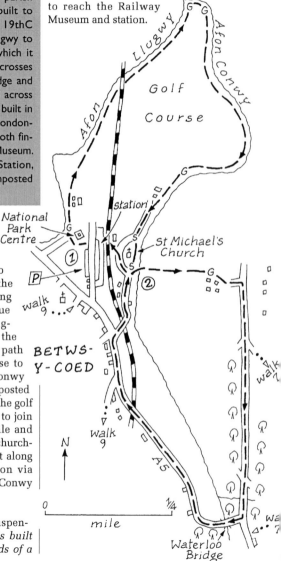

I From the car park exit opposite the clock at the railway station entrance, take a nearby pathway signposted to the National Park Centre/Tourist Information Centre. Go past the arched entrance then take the signposted path through a gate along the lane to Royal Oak Farm. Continue along a stony footpath, soon alongside the river Llugwy, to pass under the railway bridge. Follow the riverside path along the perimeter of the golf course to the confluence of the Llugwy and Conwy rivers. Continue on the regularly signposted riverside path along the other edge of the golf course, through a kissing gate, and on to join a lane. On its bend, cross a stone stile and go through the edge of St. Michael's churchyard to a road. (For **Walk B**, turn right along the road to access the railway station via the tempting Buffet Coach Café and Conwy Valley Railway Shop and Museum.)

2 For **Walk A**, cross the nearby suspension bridge over the river. *It was built in 1930, after the destruction by floods of a*

12

WALK 9

CLOGWYN GIGFRAN

DESCRIPTION A 3¾ mile walk following a waymarked forest trail through mixed woodland, with good views across both the upper Conwy and Lledr valleys. Allow about 2 hours.
START As **Walk 8**.

1 Go to the main road and turn LEFT. Go past the road signposted to the Railway Museum, then take a road on the right passing behind Cotswolds. Follow the road past Betws-y-Coed Motors and then through majestic mature woodland for about ½ mile. Just before the railway bridge, take a forestry track on the right. It rises steadily up the wooded hillside to reach a viewpoint across the wooded valley. It later passes a more extensive viewpoint over the Afon Conwy, after which it enters the Lledr valley. The track reaches an old mine and green track at Clogwyn Gigfran (Giant's Head) overlooking the river and railway line below, after which it climbs away from the valley.

2 When the track bends sharp left, turn RIGHT at a blue-topped post to follow a path, soon through an open area of woodland, across a footbridge and on through a small gate. Go across a track leading to a nearby house and alongside its fence boundary to follow the blue-topped posts angling up the slope to go through a small gate and on up to an old forestry track. Turn RIGHT. At a track junction bear RIGHT down to another junction. Bear RIGHT again, soon passing a cleared area of forest with extensive views. Shortly, the white-topped post trail from Llyn Elsi angles in from the left. Continue down the track, eventually leaving the forest to reach the road behind St. Mary's church. Follow it RIGHT down to the main road and back to the start.

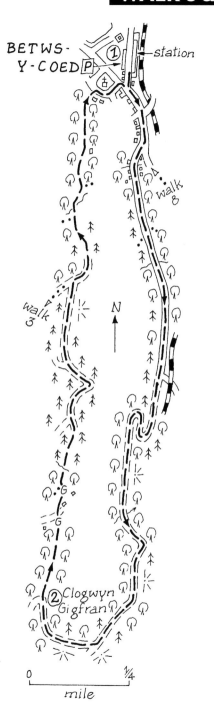

BETWS-
Y-COED ℗ ① —station

N

Walk 8

Walk 3

② Clogwyn Gigfran

0 — ¼
mile

WALK 10

LLYN PARC

DESCRIPTION A 7 mile figure of eight walk **(A)** exploring the attractive mature mixed woodland of Gwydyr Forest Park north of Betws-y-Coed, featuring the upland lake of Llyn Parc and prominent viewpoints. It combines three waymarked forest trails on good paths and tracks. The route initially crosses the wooded hillside beneath Clogwyn Cyrau escarpment before steadily climbing Aberllyn Ravine past old mine workings to reach Llyn Parc. It continues along the eastern side of the lake, then descends in stages to a car park at the start of the Marin Mountain Bike Trail. The route then heads south, later climbing to pass the end of Llyn Parc, and following another trail above Aberllyn Ravine on a steady descent, past another viewpoint. Allow about 4 hours. The route includes three shorter walks of 1½ miles **(B)**, 2¾ miles **(C)** and 4¼ miles **(D)**. Starting from the Forest car park [SH 791609] accessed from the B5106 offers a 4 1/4 mile walk to Llyn Parc.

START Pont-y-Pair, Betws-y-Coed [SH 792567].

DIRECTIONS This ancient stone bridge lies just off the A5 in the centre of Betws-y-Coed.

1 At the far side of the bridge turn LEFT on a minor road past a car park and toilets. Shortly, take a road on the right, which soon bends left up past wooden houses and becomes a stony track. Take the signposted blue and white forestry trail on the right, and at the path junction, turn RIGHT signposted 'Cyrau'. The path angles up across the wooded slope to pass beneath Clogwyn Cyrau escarpment, guided by white topped posts, to reach a viewpoint overlooking Betws-y-Coed. Follow the path through mixed woodland, later descending to a waymarked path junction. (For **Walk B** turn right and follow the yellow/white waymarked path, then track down to the road.)

2 Turn LEFT to join the Llyn Parc trail, whose yellow topped posts will guide you for the next few miles. The path rises, later more steeply up the edge of the narrowing Aberllyn Ravine above the stream to reach the top of a small waterfall. *The sealed mine entrances, debris and ruins are relics of lead and zinc mines that were worked here during the 18thC until their abandonment early last century.* After crossing a footbridge over the stream, continue along the forest edge, passing a nearby cottage to a forestry road at the end of Llyn Parc. (For **Walk C** turn left to point **5**)

3 Now follow the path along the right-hand edge of the lake, initially open, then wooded. *The water level of this sheltered remote lake is now much lower than when it provided water power for the mines. Today, despite its life-restricting high-level mineral content, it is a peaceful place to watch the dragonflies skimming its surface.* At its end, the path bends RIGHT up to the forestry road. (For **Walk D** turn right and follow the road back past the southern end of the lake to point **5**.) Follow it LEFT and at a junction, take the LEFT fork, descending with a track past side paths. At a junction of tracks, go half-RIGHT up the waymarked yellow trail. After 100 yards, leave the track to follow the waymarked trail path through the trees. After a while the path bears right and continues below a green track. Shortly, swing sharp LEFT down the yellow waymarked path to the top tier of a car park. Turn RIGHT past a Marin Mountain Bike Trail Information Board.

4 Go along the multi-use track below the start of the bike trail, soon enjoying extensive views along the Conwy Valley and across to Llanwrst. When the track splits keep on the upper fork to follow the yellow trail past side paths to reach a picnic area at a prominent viewpoint. Keep ahead at a track junction to follow the trail along the wooded hillside. After a while the track becomes a wide, then stony path, rising steadily. At a stream it bends sharp RIGHT and continues up to a forestry road. Turn LEFT along the road with glimpses of Llyn Parc to reach the end of the lake. Continue up the forestry road.

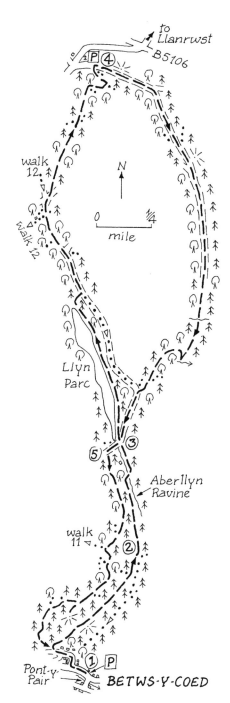

Pont-y-pair

5 Shortly, join a new blue waymarked trail on the left. The path soon descends then rises past a small ruin, before crossing a shelf giving good views across the Llugwy valley. It then briefly joins a section of the cycle route to reach a bend of the stony track. *A few yards further is a good view of Moel Siabod.* Here the path descends LEFT to reach a track below an area of cleared forest. Follow it LEFT. Shortly, the blue trail turns RIGHT. First continue ahead, and as the path begins to descend, take a path heading half-LEFT to reach a crag overlooking Betws-y-Coed. Return to follow the waymarked trail up to pass round the fenced-off corner of an old mine, where you turn LEFT to follow the waymarked path, soon descending to a post. Here, the path descends LEFT through conifers, later passing a seat to join your outward route back to the start.

LLYN SARNAU AND LLANWRST MINE ENGINE HOUSE

DESCRIPTION A 5½ mile (**A**) walk exploring Gwydyr Forest Park on good paths and tracks, incorporating part of a waymarked forest trail. The route climbs to a high viewpoint on Clogwyn Cyrau overlooking the town, before meandering across the part-wooded upland area, with extensive mountain views, to visit the 19thC Llanrwst mine engine-house, with surviving chimney, and passing Llyn Sarnau, an upland reservoir that provided water for local lead-mines. After a descent into the Llugwy valley, the route offers a road or riverside return from the Miners Bridge. Allow about 3½ hours. A shorter 4 mile walk (**B**) is included.

START Pont-y-Pair, Betws-y-Coed [SH 792567].

DIRECTIONS This ancient stone bridge lies just off the A5 in the centre of Betws-y-Coed.

I At the far side of the bridge turn LEFT on a minor road past a car park and toilets. Shortly, take a road on the right, which soon bends left up past wooden houses and becomes a stony track. Take the signposted blue and white forestry trail on the right, and at the path junction keep ahead, signposted Pen-yr-Allt (the blue trail). The path angles steeply across the wooded slope to a seat, then rises through conifers, the gradient gradually easing, to reach a green forestry post. Turn RIGHT up the blue trail to reach a fenced-off mine. Turn RIGHT and follow the trail path to a green track. Before continuing left, turn RIGHT, and shortly as the path begins to descend take a path heading half-LEFT to reach the crag on Clogwyn Cyrau overlooking Betws-y-Coed. Return to the green track and follow it through the wood. At its bend turn RIGHT to follow the blue trail path up to a stony path.

2 Here you leave the blue trail, by turning LEFT to pass a ruined house – *with a good view of Moel Siabod*. Follow the track through mixed woodland. When it splits, take the right fork, then continue ahead up the forestry track. At the next junction, turn LEFT, now rejoining the blue trail. After a while, turn LEFT off the track to follow the blue trail rising through the trees to eventually reach a forestry track. Turn LEFT to pass the dam of a small reservoir on your right to reach a track junction. (For **Walk B** turn LEFT on the signposted blue trail down a path to cross a ladder-stile. Turn RIGHT past an old barn and follow the lower green track to pass in front of Coed Mawr to cross a ladder-stile. Follow a green track to cross a stile, then a path alongside the fence. It crosses two step stiles, then a ladder-stile, before descending to a forestry track to rejoin **Walk A**. Turn LEFT and resume text at point 4.)

3 Walk A continues up the track. At the top of the rise go half-RIGHT up a side track, then follow it down past a cottage to eventually reach a track junction – *en route enjoying excellent views across the Llugwy valley to Moel Siabod, the Glyders, and the Carneddau mountains*. Turn RIGHT and follow the track past a waymarked cross-path to another forestry track. Cross the ladder-stile opposite and go along the signposted path. At a waymarker post turn RIGHT and follow the path towards the chimney to reach Llanwrst lead-mine engine house – *built in 1876/77 to pump water from the mine*. Return to the ladder-stile, then follow the track RIGHT down to a track junction. Turn LEFT and follow the track which divides Llyn Sarnau to pass a cross-track. Continue along the track, soon enjoying extensive views. Shortly, go down the right fork of the track to join the blue trail near an area of old workings.

4 Continue along the forestry track, past a side track, to reach an open aspect by a ladder-stile. A signposted path on the left leads to a nearby Sun Seat, which makes a good place for a break. Cross the ladder-stile and continue ahead, over a stile, and on along an old green track to cross another stile. Continue down past a stone barn, cross a track leading to a nearby house, and go down the path, soon bearing RIGHT to join a wall by a small white gate below the house. Follow the wall down to cross a ladder-stile into the forest. After a short steep descent requiring care, the path widens and angles steadily down through the trees to reach a road. Turn LEFT and follow the road back to the start, or take the signposted path opposite angling down to the Miners Bridge, and return along the riverside path.

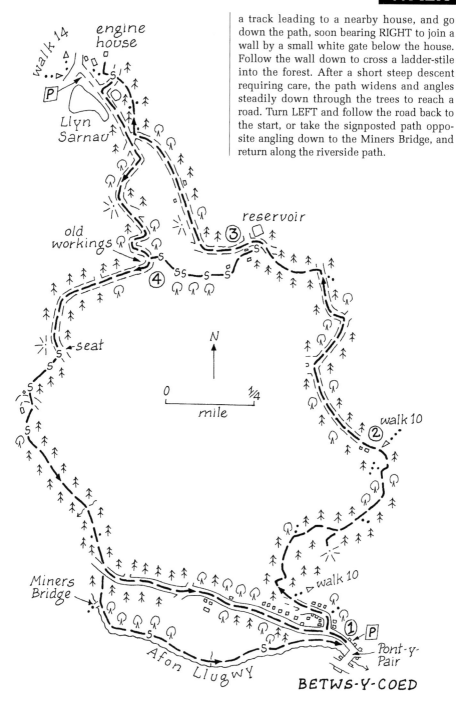

BETWS-Y-COED

WALK 12

MINERS TRAIL

DESCRIPTION A 3½ mile walk (**A**) exploring the remains of the once thriving lead-mining industry that dominated the upland slopes of what is now Gwydyr Forest. The route combines a waymarked forest trail, featuring the Hafna Mill complex and a good viewpoint, with part of a waymarked Miners Trail established by Forest Enterprise, which visits the former Parc mine site, the largest of Gwydyr's lead and zinc mines and other sites, now hidden in the forest. Interpretation panels at key locations provide further information on the mining history. These abandoned mines now provide an important habitat for hibernating and roosting bats, which are able to access the old underground workings through special open bat-capped shafts. Allow about 2 hours. It can easily be undertaken as two shorter walks of 2½ (**B**) and 1½ (**C**) miles.

START Hafna Mine car park [SH 781601]

DIRECTIONS From Betws-y-Coed, cross Pont-y-Pair and follow the B5106 north for 3 miles. Just past Gwydir Castle (worth a visit) and immediately before a junction, turn left by a forestry sign and follow a narrow road up the the wooded valley for 1¼ miles to reach the car park on the right.

Small-scale mining for lead and zinc began on the Gwydyr estate in the early 17thC, encouraged by its owner, Sir John Wynn, but it was during the 19thC that mining became more organised, employing many men. Fortunes fluctuated and by end of the century, the industry had greatly declined. High mineral prices then saw a revival with some mines re-opening until the 1920s but only Parc, the largest of the Gwydyr mines, continued, until finally closing in the early 1960s.

The Hafna Mill complex which operated between 1879 – 1915 includes a smelthouse built in the 1880s on the 3rd level. The site also contains the remains of ore bins, sorting, crushing and separation floors, thickening tanks, and a slime pit used to collect residues from the milling process. The

prominent chimney was built above the mill to remove toxic fumes formed from smelting. Ore came by an adit and a shaft on the top level.

1 Take the path leading up from the car park entrance to reach the mill complex. (For **Walk B** follow the forestry track up to point **2**). Follow the iron railing on your right past the former slime pit to an information board overlooking the car park, then take the railed stepped path up the right hand side of the complex to another information board. Continue up the stepped path passing to the right of the chimney to cross a stile. Continue up the track guided by blue-topped posts. When the track swings right, go half-RIGHT to take a path up through the trees, then follow a track up to a cross-track. Here, turn sharp RIGHT and follow the track through the forest. At a track junction, turn RIGHT. At the next junction bear RIGHT again. After 30 yards, at a green forestry post, a short diversion LEFT on a stony path leads to a viewpoint overlooking the Conwy valley. Afterwards, continue along the forestry track, past an old mine on the right, before beginning a steady descent. At a blue-topped post the track crosses a small stream. About 15 yards further, you reach a green forestry post on the left. (For **Walk C**, simply continue down the track to the start.)

2 Here, turn sharp LEFT to follow a path down through the trees to the road. Continue on the path opposite on the way-marked Miners Trail – *(the waymarks are the traditional mining tools of pick and hammer)* – later alongside a fence to reach a walled area on the site of Parc mine overlooking a side valley. *This area once contained the miners' changing room and shower block. The brown coloured streams below flow from the two main levels of the mine.* Now head up the tarmaced track to cross a stile on its bend to visit Kneebone's Cutting – *named after Capt. Kneebone, the mine manager when ore was extracted from here.* Return to continue along the track, then turn RIGHT up another tarmaced track on the waymarked trail.

3 Shortly after passing forestry tracks follow the trail half-RIGHT to pass the left-hand side of a small building, not the Marin path. Follow the waymarked path past a scree slope and the former Parc mine no. 2 level to descend through the trees, past an old building – *formerly office/stores* – then down past a circular bat-capped shaft to reach a forestry track. Turn LEFT past further mines hidden in the trees. After a while the track begins to rise, crosses a stream, and bends north. At a waymarker post the trail turns LEFT up a stony path and continues past the former Vale of Conway Mill site, featuring a crusher house and wheel-pit, later alongside a stream to reach the road. Turn RIGHT back to the start.

Hafna Mine

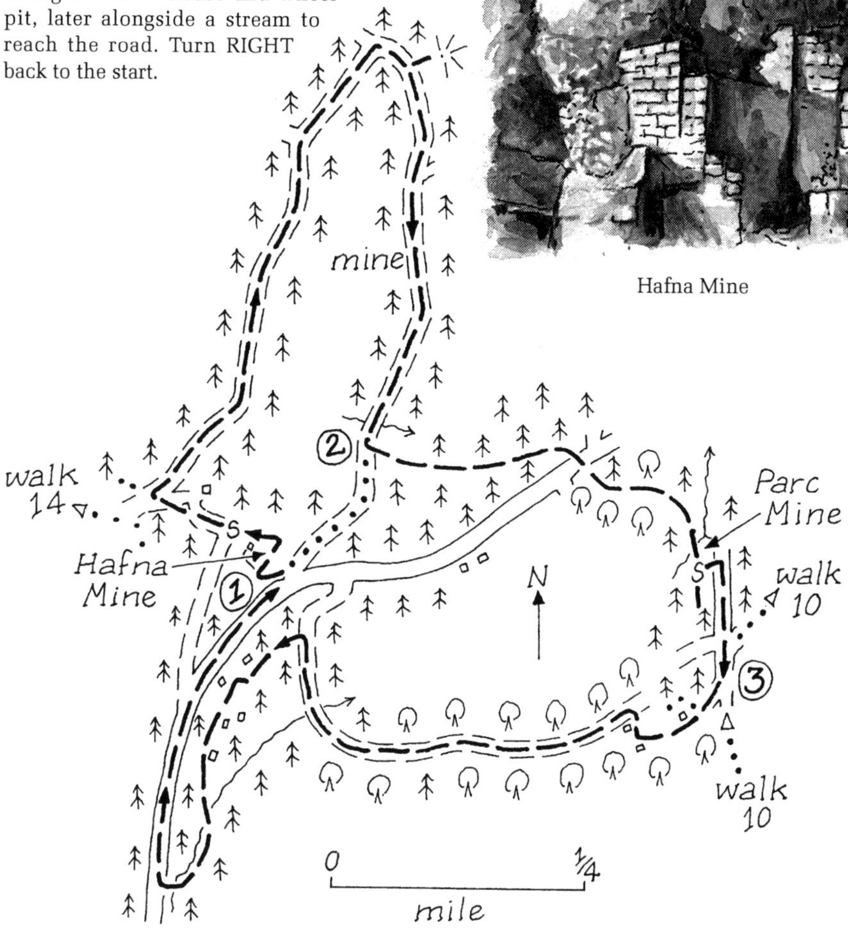

walk 14

Hafna Mine

mine

Parc Mine

walk 10

walk 10

N

0   ¼

mile

WALK 13
SWALLOW FALLS AND CYFFTY MINE

DESCRIPTION A choice of a 3½ mile **(A)** or 2½ mile **(B)** walk featuring the Llugwy gorge and the famous Swallow Falls. **Walk B** follows a yellow waymarked forest trail through the mixed woodland of Coed Cae Huddygl, steep in places, but featuring a dramatic high viewpoint looking towards Moel Siabod and Snowdon. **Walk A** initially follows the forest trail, before continuing to the Ugly House and following a riverside path to the falls. It then follows woodland and field paths up to the 19thC Cyffty leadmine, where interpretation panels provide an insight into the old mine workings, and a scenic road back to the start. Allow about 2½ hours.

START Ty'n Llwyn car park/picnic site [SH 765583]. An alternative start for **Walk B** is Cyffty mine site [SH 772589].

DIRECTIONS From Betws-y-Coed follow the A5 towards Capel Curig. After crossing the Afon Llugwy take the single-track road on the right alongside the Ugly House and follow the road up the hillside for ¾ mile to reach Ty'n Llwyn car park. The alternative start at Cyffty mine is further along the road.

I Go through a gap in the wall on the western side of the car park and across the slope past picnic tables on the Swallow Falls signposted path to cross a ladder-stile. Follow the path across the open slope guided by yellow topped posts to reach a large tree on your left. Ignore the path straight ahead, but go half-RIGHT passing to the right of a post through the bracken, soon bearing RIGHT up past another post to cross a ladder-stile near a gate adjoining the road. Follow the path into the wood, soon descending to a green forestry post at a path junction. (The path to your left is the returning trail). Keep ahead to follow the steadily descending path, en route crossing a wall, to reach a forestry track. Go half-RIGHT to continue down a

path on an easier descent across the wooded slope to reach another forestry track. (For **Walk B**, turn LEFT to take the lower right fork and follow the track, later becoming a path, to reach Swallow Falls.)

2 For **Walk A** turn RIGHT and follow the track to a road. Turn LEFT past The Towers Outdoor Education Centre down to the A5 at the Ugly House (Ty Hyll). *It is said to have originally been a 'ty unnos' – a house built between sunset and sunrise, which according to ancient law gave ownership to the builder if the chimney emitted smoke from a fire by dawn!* Turn LEFT towards the bridge to take a signposted path down steps to the riverbank then follow the shady riverside path to cross a ladder-stile. Continue close to the river and along the edge of a field to cross another ladder-stile. Follow the path along the edge of a wood, keeping close to the river to eventually reach Swallow Falls, where you rejoin **Walk B**. Follow the fenced path above the waterfall. Soon a seat below gives a fine view looking back at the falls. The path now descends above the lower falls through the mature trees clinging to the steep slope. Shortly you reach a path junction.

3 For **Walk B**, turn LEFT signposted to Ty'n Llwyn and follow the waymarked trail up through the wood. At a cross-path by the stream, turn LEFT and follow the trail path up to a forestry track. Follow it RIGHT, and shortly, take the stepped trail path on the left. The path rises, initially steeply, up the wooded slope, then lessens as it continues up through dense conifers. Where you have a glimpse of the forest edge on your right, the path bears LEFT up through the conifers, becoming less dense, and continues bending south to pass below a small crag with a superb viewpoint along the Llugwy valley. Continue along the waymarked path, soon passing through an old wall gap. Shortly, it bears RIGHT up to join your outward route, which you follow back to the start.

For **Walk A**, continue ahead down the path, shortly crossing a footbridge. After passing a green track angling in from the left, take the left fork of the path up through conifers to a finger post. Bear RIGHT down to cross

20

a footbridge. Shortly, at a path junction, turn LEFT, and after about 30 yards, just beyond the bend, turn RIGHT up a short path to emerge on an adjoining road near a cottage. Take the signposted path opposite alongside the cottage boundary to a stile. Cross a ladder-stile ahead and follow the path up through open woodland. At a stony cross-path turn RIGHT past a Marin sign. Just beyond, turn sharp LEFT to cross a stream and a stile. Continue ahead to cross a ladder-stile, then head over to the boundary and continue up the field edge, skirting round a wet reedy area, to enter an adjoining field at a ladder-stile. Headup the slope to go through an old gateway adjoining a stone barn. Follow the access track of the nearby house to cross a ladder-stile. Continue up the track and just before the next stone building go half-LEFT across the grass to cross a ladder-stile. Take the waymarked path ahead to cross a ladder-stile at the former Cyffty lead-mine.

4 Go up the path, then turn LEFT to an information panel by a ruin and wheelpit. *The lead-mine, established in the 1850s, was worked from two shafts, with ore being extracted from the Engine Shaft, primarily by horsepower. The wheelpit once housed a 35ft waterwheel, which originally provided power for pumping water from the mine, then after 1920 helped power a new mineral dressing plant. Buildings below the car park-*

Ugly House

ing area date from the 1870s and included a crushing-mill, blacksmiths, and mine office. Continue along the fenced path past another wheelpit to the mine's Western Shaft. Return to the main path and follow it up across a track to the road. Turn LEFT and follow the road back to Ty'n Llwyn car park.

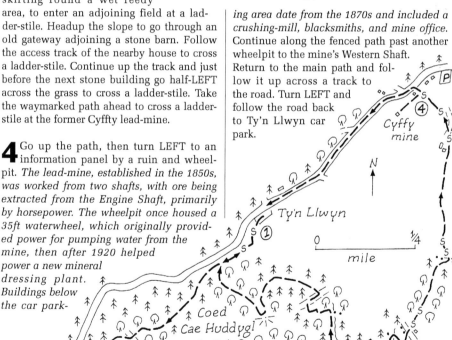

GWYDYR LAKES TRAIL

DESCRIPTION A 5½ mile walk (**A**), with extensive views, exploring an area of Gwydyr Forest Park featuring numerous scenic upland lakes that once provided water for the lead-mines. The route incorporates a 2 mile way-marked forest trail (**B**) and includes an optional additional ¾ mile walk (**C**) to the 19thC Llanwrst mine engine house, returning past Llyn Sarnau. The route follows the yellow forest trail to delightful little known upland lakes, then leaves the trail to pass Llyn Glangors and cross upland pasture to go along the eastern shore of Llyn Geirionydd. After diverting to Llyn Bodgynydd, it then rejoins the forest trail. Allow about 3½ hours.

START Llyn Sarnau car park [SH 778592].

DIRECTIONS Follow directions in **Walk 12** to Hafna mine car park, then continue up the road past Nant-B.H. Outdoor Education Centre to reach a car park on the left by Llyn Sarnau.

I At the far end of the car park are two paths leading into the forest opposite. Take the right one signposted to Llyn Glangors. Follow the path through the forest guided by yellow-topped posts. After a while the path splits, where you bend RIGHT with the yellow trail, briefly descending, then contouring through the tall trees. At a green forestry post, the path does a U-turn. *Nearby is a good viewpoint. Take care – keep away from the edge.* Soon, turn RIGHT along a forestry track.

2 After several bends, the yellow trail turns LEFT off the track up through a clearing. The path passes a mine shaft on the right, then another mine, and continues to a track. Follow it LEFT past a small attractive lake. Shortly, the trail turns RIGHT to pass between the first lake and a larger one, then bears LEFT along its northern side and on to reach a forestry track. Turn RIGHT. (For **Walk B**, then turn LEFT down a path to a forestry track. Follow it LEFT past another lake and

on to a viewpoint with seats at point **5**.)

3 For **Walk A** continue down the track, shortly enjoying views of Llyn Glangors and the other lake passed on the trail. At a telegraph pole, turn sharp LEFT down a path to cross a ladder-stile. Go across the end of the lake and up to a rise by a telegraph pole. Continue down the slope, past another telegraph pole, to cross a ladder-stile. Continue ahead towards the distant mountains soon following the line of telegraph poles down to cross another ladder-stile. Head half-RIGHT towards the lower of two concrete buildings on the site of the former New Pandora lead mine, then turn RIGHT up a track. At the end of the second building, turn LEFT along the fence to go through a gateway in it, and on over a nearby ladder-stile. Follow the clear path across pasture, soon angling steadily down across the bracken-covered hillside towards Llyn Geirionydd to join a road.

4 Turn LEFT to follow the road along the eastern side of the lake, past a slipway and car park/toilets. *Llyn Geirionydd is said to be the home of the 6thC poet Talisien. Trees were planted here in 1929 to soften the landscape scarred by intensive mining in the 1870s. The car park stands on the waste tip and the adjacent mine level were part of the New Pandora mine complex. Lead was taken by tramway along the eastern shore of the lake then by aerial ropeway to Klondike lead mill mine 250 feet below. The mill was powered by water from the lake.* Continue along the road past the end of the lake. Shortly, it turns up a side valley, later passing a large area of spoil heaps and a signposted path along a track leading to Ty'n-y-Groes. You then pass a forest and a signposted path into it. Continue up the road for a further 60 yards, then go through a small gate at a parking area on your right, giving access to Cors Bodgynyd Nature Reserve. Follow the stony path, soon passing a delightful small lake and an old mine. Continue along the path, soon reaching Llyn Bodgynydd – *a reservoir for the Pandora lead-mine.* The path continues along its southern edge. *Opposite a tiny island on the shoreline is a memorial seat.* Return to the road and take an unsigned path opposite. Follow this good path up the mixed wooded hillside to reach a forestry track where you rejoin the yellow trail. Turn RIGHT past seats.

5 Continue along the track, then on a bend, at a fenced-off mine and a green forestry post, turn LEFT up a green track to reach another forestry track. Follow it RIGHT past a house and a side track, soon with good views across a cleared forest to another small lake. At a track junction turn LEFT, past a path

Shortly, cross a ladder-stile on the left. Go up the path,then turn RIGHT to reach a way-marked path junction. Take the left fork to the Llanwrst mine engine house. Follow the waymarked path past it, soon bearing RIGHT to cross a ladder-stile. Turn RIGHT down the track, then turn LEFT down another forestry track opposite a ladder-stile/finger post. Shortly, at a cross-path, turn RIGHT down to the forestry road. Follow it RIGHT past Llyn Sarnau back to the start.

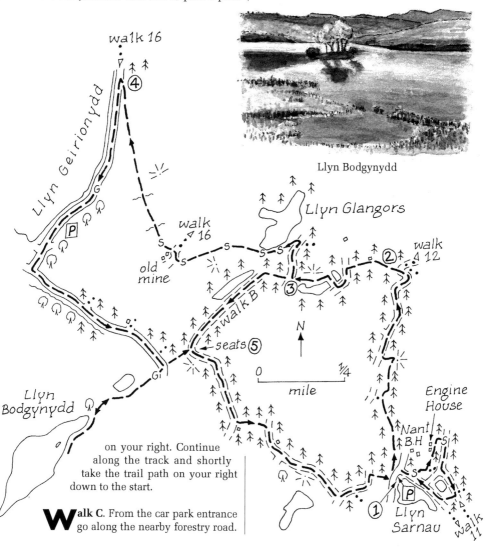

Llyn Bodgynydd

on your right. Continue along the track and shortly take the trail path on your right down to the start.

W alk C. From the car park entrance go along the nearby forestry road.

23

LLYN CRAFNANT AND LLYN GEIRIONYDD

DESCRIPTION A 5¼ mile walk (**A**) visiting two popular beautiful scenic upland lakes, enclosed by hills and mountains, or an easy 3 mile circuit of Llyn Crafnant (**B**). The route follows a track along the side of Llyn Crafnant and beyond, then joins the valley road, before taking a path up across a forested ridge and down into the adjoining valley. It then follows a lakeside path, uneven in parts due to exposed tree roots, along the western side of Llyn Geirionydd (there is an equally enjoyable road alternative), before crossing part-wooded slopes past an old mine down to the start. Allow about 3½ hours. An alternative 2 mile circuit of Llyn Geirionydd can be enjoyed starting from the lakeside car park. **START** Crafnant Forestry car park [SH 756618]. **DIRECTIONS** From the centre of Trefriw, take the road signposted to Llyn Crafnant opposite Gwesty Fairy Falls Hotel. Follow the narrow road up past junctions for nearly 2 miles to reach the car park/toilets, 200 metres below the head of the lake.

I From the information board at the western end of the car park, follow the signposted Llyn Crafnant path up through the trees to the road. Continue up the road above Afon Crafnant to reach the lake. *Just ahead is a monument erected in 1896 by inhabitants of Llanwrst to commemorate the gift by Richard James of the lake, created into a reservoir for the town.* Turn RIGHT across the lake's outlet, through a kissing gate, then follow the track along the northern side of the lake towards the craggy head of the valley. When the track splits keep to the lower fork. Shortly after passing the end of the lake the track becomes a stony path, which rises steadily to a waymarked path junction.

2 Here, take the left fork down to a ladder-stile below, near the stream, and follow the path down through the conifers to go through a gate and across a footbridge by Hendre Bach. Turn LEFT, go through a gate, across a stream, then follow the track down beneath a house, past the wooden cottage of Tan-y-Manod, and on to go through a gate at the end of the tarmaced valley road. Continue along the road, past a house – *soon with good views along the lake* – then the properties of Pen-y-Llyn and Cornel.

3 At a stone building just before a telephone box, take the signposted Geirionydd path on the right. After crossing a ladder-stile, the path angles across the slope beneath trees, crosses a stream, then, at a path junction, bends sharp RIGHT to climb steadily up through conifers guided by occasional blue-topped posts. The path eventually levels out, passes through a wall and begins a descent into the next valley. Just below it meets a forestry track. Keep ahead, and at the track junction, turn RIGHT, then take a path on the left down through the trees to the forestry track. Continue ahead down the path (can be muddy – use track if necessary), cross the forestry track again to follow the path down to rejoin the forestry track, which takes you down towards Llyn Geirionydd.

4 On the bend, where the track levels out, cross a stile ahead beneath a cottage. (Alternatively, keep with the track, then follow the road alongside the lake. At its head, go through a kissing gate and follow a track to rejoin the main route at point **5** by the monument.) Follow the path, soon alongside Llyn Geirionydd to cross a stile at a wood corner. The path keeps close to the wooded edge of the lake, later climbing a small rocky spur above a corner of the lake, before descending near a fence enclosing an old mine to continue along the lakeside. After a stile, follow the waymarked path alongside the wall up to reach a green track by a stone building. Take the waymarked path up to the nearby monument – *erected in 1850 to commemorate the reputed birthplace of Talisien, a 6thChief Bard. It was toppled in a 1976 storm, then re-erected in*

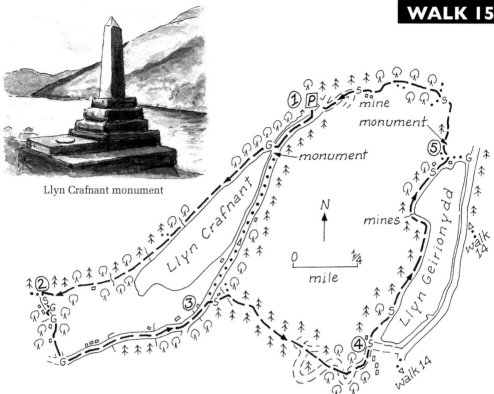

Llyn Crafnant monument

1994. In summer, parties of Victorian visitors came here, often entertained by music and sports. Between 1863-1922, an annual poetry/musical event, first established by local poet Gwilym Cowyld, was held at the monument.

5 Descend its far side to continue on the waymarked path past trees and through a wall-gap. Follow the waymarked Trefriw Trails path down to cross a ladder-stile. Just ahead, bear RIGHT on the waymarked trail, keeping ahead at the next junction across the part-wooded slope to go through a wall-gap. The trail path now rises, soon bearing RIGHT at a path junction and continues across the slope, with views into the Crafnant valley to reach an old mine site. *Slate was extracted from the hillside from the 18thC until the early 20thC.* Continue down the path, over a stile, then follow a forestry track down to the road by the car park.

About the author, David Berry

David is an experienced walker with a love of the countryside and an interest in local history. He is the author of a series of walks guidebooks covering North Wales, where he has lived and worked for many years, as well as a freelance writer for Walking Wales magazine. He has worked as a Rights of Way surveyor across North Wales and is a member of Denbighshire Local Access Forum. Whether on a riverside ramble, mountain or long distance walk, he greatly appreciates the beauty, culture and history of the landscape and hopes that his comprehensive guidebooks will encourage people to explore on foot its diverse scenery and rich heritage.

LLYN GEIRIONYDD & LLANRHYCHWYN CHURCH

DESCRIPTION A 7 mile walk featuring a popular lake above Trefriw and the remote upland Llanrhychwyn church, said to be the oldest in Wales. The route passes the Fairy Falls, then climbs steadily to cross the part-wooded slopes above Cwm Crafnant to follow an old tramway to Llyn Geirionydd. The route completes a near circuit of the lake via path, uneven in parts due to exposed tree roots, and road before rising to the former New Pandora lead-mine, then continuing to the church, with an alternative mines route described. Allow about 4 hours. The upland country road offers shorter route options.
START Car park, Trefriw [SH 782630] See Walk 19.

*L*lanrhychwyn church, *dating from the late 11th/early 12thC, stands on the site of an 'enclosure' ('llan'), a simple church made of wood or wattle, established in the 6thC by the Celtic saint Rhychwyn. For centuries people have worshipped by candlelight in this charming church, including Llywelyn the Great. Legend says that his wife Joan, daughter of King John of England, despaired of the tiring climb to the church, so in 1230 he had St. Mary's church built in Trefriw for her. In the 19thC, this upland parish was extensively worked for lead, zinc and slate, which were shipped from a quay at Trefriw.*

I Go to the woollen mill and turn RIGHT over the bridge, then take the first road on the left. After 20 yards, take a signposted path on the left to the river. Go past a footbridge, through a kissing gate, and on past lower Fairy Falls. Follow the path under a bridge, past a seat and up to cross this bridge. Turn RIGHT along a path above the river to a road. Turn RIGHT, then at the junction, LEFT up the road. Shortly, take a sign-posted path on the right (*Trefriw Trails 5*). Follow the path up through the wood, over a stile, and past a path junction. Follow the waymarked trail across the wooded, then more open hillside, up to a good viewpoint. After a small gate it crosses a stream to reach an open section above Klondike Mill. *Lead and zinc ore was taken by tramway along Llyn Geirionydd's eastern shore from the New Pandora mine (now a car park), then by aerial ropeway from here to the mill 250 feet below for processing. The mill was powered by water from the lake.* Continue along the former tramway, crossing two ladder-stiles to reach the road.

2 Just before the lake go through a kiss-ing gate and follow a track across its outlet. *The monument ahead was erected in 1850 to commemorate the reputed birth-place of Talisien, a Chief Bard of the 6thC. Destroyed in a 1976 storm, it was re-erected in 1994.* Just past a stone building, turn LEFT to follow a path alongside a wall down to the lake. Continue on the lakeside path, past old mines, across a small spur at the lake corner, and on through conifers, then a meadow to reach a forestry track near a house. Follow it LEFT to a road. Turn LEFT and follow the lakeside road past the car park/toilets.

3 At a gate across the road at a forest cor-ner, take the signposted path on the right. It angles up across the bracken-covered hillside and upland pasture to cross a ladder-stile. Turn LEFT, then go through a gateway in the fence on your right. Turn LEFT along-side the fence past the site of the former New Pandora lead mine to reach a track. Turn LEFT through a gate. Follow the track up to Castell-y-Gwynt, then the stiled path past the house. Continue alongside its garden wall and on up to go through a gate – *with a view of Llyn Glangors.*

4 Here you have a choice. (For the mines route keep ahead, and after 60 yards go half-RIGHT to follow a path near the bound-ary to cross a stile into the forest. The stiled path now alternates inside, outside and again inside the forest boundary before descend-ing past mines and spoiltips to eventually reach a forestry track. Follow it LEFT to a farmhouse and a link path up to the church.) For the direct route to the church, head half-LEFT up the slope, soon passing a reedy area to reach a rise – *with extensive mountain views*. Go down alongside an old wall, past a small ruin to cross a ladder-stile. Keep ahead, soon bearing half-LEFT to follow a path down through a reedy area, then between two small grassy ridges to cross a ladder-stile in the wall below. The path descends through an area of young trees, crosses a ladder-stile and continues to cottages. Go along their access track.

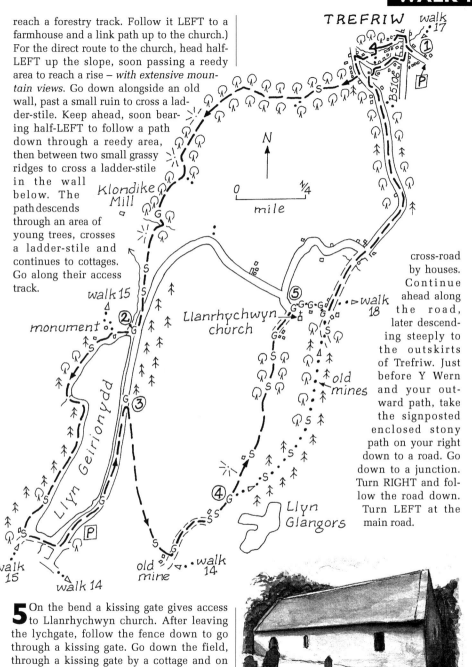

cross-road by houses. Continue ahead along the road, later descending steeply to the outskirts of Trefriw. Just before Y Wern and your outward path, take the signposted enclosed stony path on your right down to a road. Go down to a junction. Turn RIGHT and follow the road down. Turn LEFT at the main road.

5 On the bend a kissing gate gives access to Llanrhychwyn church. After leaving the lychgate, follow the fence down to go through a kissing gate. Go down the field, through a kissing gate by a cottage and on down to another kissing gate. Descend the path to a track by a farmhouse. Turn LEFT and follow the access track, then road to a

Llanrhychwyn Church

27

LLANWRST – TREFRIW VALLEY WALK

DESCRIPTION A 4¾ mile figure of eight level walk between two historic communities, partly along the Conwy and Crafnant rivers. Allow about 2½ hours. The route can be undertaken as a 3 mile walk from Trefriw or a 1¾ mile walk from Llanwrst.
START Plas yn Dre car park, Llanwrst [SH 796618] or car park, Trefriw [SH 782630].
DIRECTIONS The car park, near the library and police station, is signposted off the A470 just north of Llanwrst centre. See **Walk 19** for the alternative start.

*L*anwrst *is an ancient market town known for the making of harps and clocks, and in the 19thC, the spinning of woollen yarn and the knitting of stockings. Pont Mawr was designed by the famous architect Indigo Jones and built in 1636, at an expense of £1,000 shared jointly by Caernarvon and Denbigh counties. Nearby Gwydir Castle, dating from the 16thC, was the seat of the influential Wynn family.*

I Return to the main road in Llanwrst and turn LEFT, then take the road angling off towards the railway station. Shortly, turn LEFT to follow a lane to cross a suspension bridge over the Afon Conwy. *This is a mid-20thC replacement for the original wooden Gower's Bridge, named after the Rev. John Gower, who also built the lane ahead in the 1880s to provide a link, financed by tolls levied, between Trefriw and Llanrwst railway station. Fishing was popular with Victorian visitors, and coracles were a common sight on the river.* Cross a stile on the right and follow the path along the top of the flood embankment, later leaving the Afon Conwy to run alongside the Afon Crafnant towards Trefriw. Go past a footbridge, through a kissing gate and briefly along a track, before following a path past toilets to a minor road below Trefriw woollen mill.

2 Follow the road LEFT past Plas Meirion Caravan Park, then follow a waymarked Trefriw Trails path between the Recreation Ground and a playground, then parallel with the lane, later joining it to reach the suspension bridge. Cross the stile on the right and follow the embankment path. After two further stiles, the path turns LEFT to cross a nearby stile and stream. Follow the stiled path along the edge of four fields, then a hedge-lined green track to the road behind Tu Hwnt I'r Bont. Cross Pont Mawr, then turn LEFT to follow the signposted riverside path back to the car park.

WALK 18

GRINLLWM

DESCRIPTION A 8 mile walk of great variety exploring the Conwy valley and its part-wooded edges between Llanwrst and Trefriw, featuring gentle riverside walking, two waterfalls, a short steep climb to the outlying hill of Grinllwm with good views, and the remote ancient Llanrhychwyn church (See **Walk 16** for information). Allow about 4½ hours. Two alternative returns to Llanwrst are indicated.
START Plas yn Dre car park, Llanwrst [SH 796618] or car park, Trefriw [SH 782630].

I Follow instructions in section **1** of **Walk 17** to Trefriw.

2 Join the nearby main road at the woollen mill. Turn RIGHT across the bridge, and take the first road on the left. After 20 yards, take a signposted path on the left to the river. Go past a footbridge, through a kissing gate, and on past lower Fairy Falls. Follow the path under a bridge, past a seat and up to cross this bridge. Keep ahead to reach a road. Continue up Jubileee Road and on the bend follow the waymarked path up to a road. Turn RIGHT, then just past Y Wern, take a signposted path on the left. Follow the path steadily up through the wood to cross a stile.

3 About 100 yards further, at a Trails 5 waymarker post, take the minor path angling up the wooded slope. After about

250 yards, it climbs more steeply, briefly close to a wall on
your right, up the now bracken-covered slope, then wide

down the road past a signposted path (an
alternative return route).
After a further ½ mile,
cross a ladder-stile on
the left to see the Grey
Mare's Tail waterfall
just below in Coed
Felin Blwm (anoth-
er return option).
Continue along the
road to the junc-
tion.

TREFRIW

Fairy Falls

Walk 16

Grinllwm

WALK 17

WALK
18

Llanrhychwyn
church

Walk 16

N

0 _____ ¼
mile

Afon Crafnant

Afon Conwy

station

LLANRWST

B5106

Pont
Mawr

Gwydir
Castle

chapel

waterfall

gully to cross a ladder-stile at the
top. Follow the fence to a gate in it.
Here you can simply continue with
the fence down to a track, then follow
it left. Alternatively, follow a path leading left up to the top of Grinllwm – *a new
designated open access area* – for all-round
views, then descend south, later following
a good path down above a wall to join the
track. Follow it to a road. Turn RIGHT. At the
junction, keep ahead. On the bend a kissing
gate gives access to Llanrhychwyn church.
From the lychgate, follow the fence down to
go through a kissing gate. Go down the field,
through a kissing gate by a cottage and on
down to another kissing gate. Descend the
path to a track by a farmhouse. Turn LEFT
past outbuildings.

4 At a cottage on your left, turn RIGHT
on a signed path through a gate. Follow
a green track through another gate, over a
stream to a stile. Continue ahead to a stile in
the wood corner. Follow a track through the
wood to a stile. Keep ahead, cross a ladder-
stile and continue to the road. Turn RIGHT

5 Go along the track
opposite towards the
forestry car park, taking its
right fork through the top tier past the Marin
cycle trail information board. Go along the
multi-user track. When it splits continue on
the higher right fork (yellow trail). After ¼
mile, at a white-topped post, turn LEFT on
a path angling down through the trees to a
road, which you follow to the B5106 below.
Turn RIGHT and after about 120 yards cross
a ladder-stile on the left. Go down the field
edge, then follow the riverside path to Pont
Mawr. Cross the bridge and turn LEFT to follow the signposted riverside path back to the
car park.

COED CREIGIAU AND CEFN CYFARWYDD

their peak bringing up to 1000 people a day along the river from Conwy, Llandudno and Deganwy. Of various industries once dependent on the river Crafnant, including a corn-mill, sawmill, and forge which made hammers/chisels for the slate quarries, only the woollen mill survives.

DESCRIPTION An exhilarating 8 mile walk (**A**) exploring the little known upland area north west of Trefriw, utilising scenic upland roads offering extensive views. The route incorporates a new waymarked woodland circuit of Coed Cregiau, which makes a less demanding shorter 2¼ mile walk (**B**), and could be extended to Llyn Cowlyd, adding 1¾ miles to the overall distance. After the woodland trail and a section of road walking, the route heads along the edge of Cwm Ddu past a remote ruined chapel and abandoned upland farms, requiring careful navigation over occasionally wet reedy terrain. It then follows the narrow Llyn Cowlyd access road over Cefn Cyfarwydd, reaching a height of 1398ft, for a dramatic descent with breathtaking views. Allow about 4½ hours. Not recommended in poor visibility.

START Car park, Trefriw [SH 782630].

DIRECTIONS A minor road opposite Trefriw woollen mill leads to a car parking area on the right near Plas Meirion Caravan Park.

Until the arrival of the railway in the 1860s, Trefriw was an important inland port serving the valley. In the first half of the 19thC vessels carried coal, lime and general goods up the river, and returned to the coast full of slate, lead ore and timber from the surrounding hills. It was also an important cloth-weaving centre. A fulling mill, taking woven cloth from cottages to wash and finish, was established in 1820. It then developed into the woollen mill, whose products are as popular today as in Victorian/ Edwardian times when Trefriw became a fashionable spa resort. The curative properties of the sulphor and iron-rich waters of the chalybeate wells, to the north of the village, known since Roman times, attracted many visitors. Passenger steamer services developed and ran until World War II – at

1 Go to the main road by the woollen mill and turn RIGHT over the river. Take the first road on the left and follow it up past side roads, then turn RIGHT up a road sign-posted to the cemetery and Llyn Cowlyd. Shortly, turn RIGHT on a waymarked 'Trefriw Trails' path up a track into Coed Creigiau, an area of mixed woodland. When it splits take the waymarked right fork. After passing a good viewpoint looking down to the river Conwy, the waymarked trail turns LEFT up through the trees, soon following a cross-path up to a forestry track. Follow it RIGHT, then turn LEFT up another track. Shortly, the trail angles off the track to pass a seat with a stunning view across the Conwy valley to Llanrwst, then bears RIGHT up to rejoin the forestry track. Follow it LEFT past a 'Sun Seat' path and a waymarker post to a road.

(For **Walk B**, at the waymark post, follow the trail path back into the wood, soon running just above the road. At a bend, follow the waymarked path, initially through tall pines, to turn right down a cross-path to join a stony track. Follow it right to rejoin your outward route.)

2 Turn RIGHT and follow the road up to a junction. Here, turn RIGHT signposted to Tyddyn Wylyn Ardda. Follow this delightful road as it contours the valley edge, enjoying increasingly extensive views along the Conwy valley. After a while the road rises past two houses and continues past two signposted paths on the right – *with pipelines running along Cwm Ddu beneath Moel Eilio prominent ahead.* The road then gently descends to cross a cattle-grid by a large modern house and continues down towards farm buildings. Keep ahead on the higher of two tracks to pass between a red-bricked barn and a large corrugated shed. Follow the track through a small wood and on past a graveyard and ruined

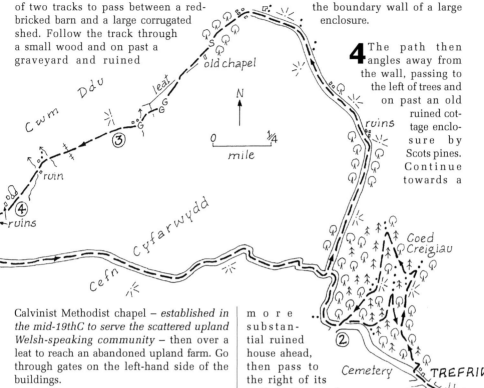

the boundary wall of a large enclosure.

4 The path then angles away from the wall, passing to the left of trees and on past an old ruined cottage enclosure by Scots pines. Continue towards a

Calvinist Methodist chapel – *established in the mid-19thC to serve the scattered upland Welsh-speaking community* – then over a leat to reach an abandoned upland farm. Go through gates on the left-hand side of the buildings.

3 Follow the faint green track alongside the fence and through the left of two gates near a stone barn. Continue up the old reedy track. When it fades at the top of the rise by boulders contour ahead across the open ground, past an old boulder wall on your right. Shortly, you will pick up a path which takes you across the intermittent gorse/bracken/reedy ground to go through an old gateway in a fence. Continue ahead across the wettish ground passing just to the left of a tree-encrusted small boulder escarpment, then the remains of a boulder wall to cross a stream. About 70 yards further, at the remains of a stone sheepfold on your right, join a path angling half-LEFT up the slope. At a tiny ruin, ignore the path close to it, but cross the stream just ahead. After 15 yards, bear half-LEFT to follow a path up across reedy ground to pass just to the right of a boulder covered mound and on through the reeds, passing to the left of a tree, then

more substantial ruined house ahead, then pass to the right of its outbuilding and work your way across the reedy ground, after 100 yards bearing half-LEFT to cross the old fence at a large old walled enclosure. Follow the old wall round and continue down the rough field for about 50 yards, then head half-LEFT through tussocks and gorse to cross a visible ladder-stile. Head nearly half-LEFT up to pass just to the right of a tree, and on past the end of a walled enclosure. Cross a small slab bridge over a stream and a gate by a ruin to reach the nearby road. (For Llyn Cowlyd, turn right.)

5 Turn LEFT and follow the road up to a dramatic viewpoint. As you descend, Llyn Geirionydd comes into view. Eventually you rejoin your outward route. At the entrance to Coed Creigiau you can complete the trail route through the forest or simply follow the road down past the cemetery.

31

PORTH-LLWYD FALLS

DESCRIPTION A demanding but interesting 3 mile walk ascending the steep hidden wooded slopes above Dolgarrog, returning past Porth-llwyd waterfall, popular with Victorian visitors, and incorporating a short informative waymarked trail commemorating the worst dam disaster in Welsh history. On 2nd November 1925 the dam of Llyn Eigau, which supplied power to generate electricity, was breached, and water cascaded down the hillside destroying part of Dolgarrog and killing 16 people. Allow about 2 hours. It links to **Walk 21** offering an easy ½ mile extension to Coedty reservoir.
START Dolgarrog [SH 769677].
DIRECTIONS Park in a side road just off the B5106 opposite the Dolgarrog and District Social Club.

another house, take a signposted path on the left. It rises across the wooded slope to join another path just below a house. Pass between the house and outbuilding to follow a meandering path up through the trees, past a path on the right, to a waymarked tree just before a ladder-stile. Follow the path bearing RIGHT to bend LEFT alongside a wall. Continue up the enclosed path – *once a highway* – passing ruins. It then contours across the wooded slope, before rising steadily past a path on the right and a small ruin to the entrance to Llidiart Fadog. Turn RIGHT and follow the lane for ¹/₃ mile up to a road. Turn LEFT up the road over a leat. Later, after crossing the leat again, follow the road down.

2 On a bend, take a signposted path over a ladder-stile (or first continue to Pont Newydd or Coedty reservoir). Go along the edge of two fields to cross a ladder-stile and another, further ahead. Bear LEFT down to go through a wall-gap. Follow the lower path

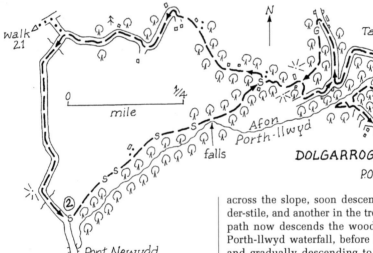

across the slope, soon descending to a ladder-stile, and another in the trees below. The path now descends the wooded gorge past Porth-llwyd waterfall, before bending away and gradually descending to a ladder-stile to join your outward route. Follow the path down the top of the wood below the house, and take the path bearing RIGHT down to a lane. Follow it LEFT down to Ceunant and return along your outward route, then follow the memorial trail, returning down a lane to the side road.)

1 Walk north along the B5106 past the start of the disaster commemorative trail, then turn LEFT along a lane. Follow it up through a wood to Ceunant, a pottery, at a junction. Bend RIGHT with the lane. When behind

WALK 21

CWM PORTH-LLWYD

DESCRIPTION A 5½ mile (**A**) or 7 mile (**B**) walk, with extensive views, exploring remote upland valleys, where man left his mark early in the 20thC in the form of water pipes and leats, and 2ft narrow gauge railways used in the construction of several reservoir dams. The route follows one such railway past Coedty reservoir and along the edge of Cwm Porth-llwyd. **Walk A** then crosses Moel Eilio ridge for a return along the upper edge of Cwm Ddu, utilising existing rights of way and a short section of open access land. **Walk B** continues to Llyn Eigiau then returns via track and open upland roads, with a path option shown. It provides a less demanding steady walk among open mountain scenery. Allow about 3½ hours. **Walk B** can be started and varied from an alternative upland car park. Both walks combine well with **Walk 20** for a Dolgarrog start.

START Pont Newydd [SH759671] or car park near Llyn Eigiau [SH 732663].

DIRECTIONS In Tal-y-Bont, turn off the B5106 on an unsigned minor road near the school. It rises steeply, through sharp bends to reach a junction after 1 mile. (For the alternative car park continue on the road for a further 2 miles to its end.) Turn left for ½ mile to find limited parking just beyond Pont Newydd.

through Coed Dolgarrog, operated between 1907-1910 during the building of Llyn Eigiau dam. Its lower section, linked with a Llyn Cowlyd railway, was used in the building of Coedty dam in 1924 and in its subsequent rebuilding. After about 2 miles you go through a gate after crossing a stream.

2 Shortly, for **Walk A**, cross a ladder-stile on the left. (For **Walk B** cross a ladder-stile ahead and follow the track to Llyn Eigiau, then another past the dam, across its outlet and along the valley to the car park. Follow the road, past an alternative path option, to the junction. Turn right back to the start.) Follow the green track up the hillside and on past an abandoned cottage to cross a stream and ladder-stile. The path rises to another ladder-stile, then crosses the slope before passing over the shoulder of Moel Eilio. Here the path splits. Take the LEFT fork. It steadily descends-with a view of Llyn Cowlyd- to a ladder-stile. Turn LEFT and follow the fence down to a gate and another ladder-stile above the pipeline. Follow a path down, soon bearing LEFT up to cross a stream at a wall/fence corner. Follow the path up to pass a ruin and across reedy upland pasture to pass

I Continue along the road, under a pipeline and up to cross a leat, where the road ends. Bear RIGHT through a gate and follow a track past Coedty reservoir, through woodland, over a leat and along the expansive Cwm Porth-llwyd beneath Moel Eilio. *This former 2ft gauge railway, which followed the route of a 19thC slate tramway connecting Llyn Cedryn quarry Eigiau with an incline*

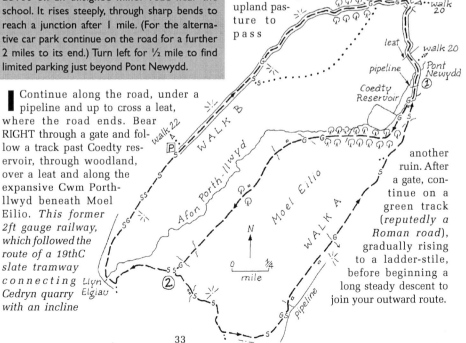

another ruin. After a gate, continue on a green track (reputedly a Roman road), gradually rising to a ladder-stile, before beginning a long steady descent to join your outward route.

PEN-Y-GAER, LLYN DULYN AND LLYN MELYNLLYN

DESCRIPTION An exhilarating 10 mile figure of eight walk, with extensive views, from Pen-y-gaer Iron Age hillfort overlooking the Conwy valley across wild upland valley and mountain landscape to visit remote lakes, used as reservoirs, set in two of the most dramatic corries in Snowdonia, beneath the central Carneddau mountain ridge. After visiting the hillfort, the route follows a delightful track to cross the Afon Ddu, after which mainly level paths across wettish ground take you to Llyn Dulyn, where there is a bothy nearby for shelter. A short steep climb to Llyn Melynllyn, at 2,094ft, is followed by a scenic high-level track, then another takes you to a small dam, after which you follow paths, later well waymarked. The route follows existing rights of way and a few well used link paths in an area designated open access land . Although, the walk starts high and involves little demanding climbing, it is for experienced walkers only, and should not be undertaken in poor visibility. Allow between 5-6 hours. The route can be shortened to a 5 mile walk (**B**) or a 5¾ mile walk (**C**) from the alternative upland car park also accessed from Tal-y-Bont (See **Walk 21**).

START Pen-y-gaer [SH 744693] or car park, near Llyn Eigiau [SH 732663].

DIRECTIONS From the Bedol pub in Tal-y-Bont, take the road signposted to Llanbedr-y-cennin. Go past the Olde Bull Inn and continue up the hillside, enjoying extensive views. At a junction, turn left and follow the road up below the northern slopes of Pen-y-Gaer to its end, where it becomes two tracks and there is a parking area near a seat.

I From the road end take the track leading south to cross a ladder-stile on the left. A clear path takes you to another ladder-stile

providing access to the hillfort. *Its defences included the rare 'cheveux de frise' – angled pointed stones embedded in the ground.* Retrace your steps, then follow the other track, soon rising to cross an old leat and a ladder-stile. Follow the track rising gently alongside the wall beneath Penygadair, over another ladder-stile, and past one on your left (your return route). The track continues across the open slopes up to a ladder-stile, then rises steadily past another ladder-stile, where it levels out, and begins a long steady descent. *Ahead in the distance, below the Carneddau ridge, are the imposing dark crags, beneath which are the hidden lakes you seek.* After a ladder-stile, continue ahead on the now faint green track, shortly beginning another long descent. Later the track fades again as it passes through a wet area to a ladder-stile.

2 After crossing the nearby river, turn LEFT and work your way across wettish ground above the river alongside the fence, which later becomes a wall, to an iron ladder-stile. (For **Walk B**, cross it and resume text at point **5**.) Here, turn RIGHT to follow a path S.W. along the edge of a line of rushes to cross a footbridge. Continue ahead to cross an iron ladder-stile in a fence. Ultimately you are aiming to pass to the right of a small group of trees ahead. In the meanwhile, continue ahead guided by occasional small concrete 'cable below' posts. Cross a stream, then another by an old stone sheepfold and continue to a ladder-stile. Keep ahead for about 150 yards, first passing above large boulders, then over two small streams. Now bear LEFT to cross a larger stream coming from the high ground ahead and go across a shoulder into Cwm Melynllyn to join a good path passing above the Scots pines. Follow it along the valley edge to pass above Dulyn bothy to reach Llyn Dulyn. *Lying beneath the near vertical crags of Craig y Dulyn which have claimed the lives of airmen, this dark lake is said to be 189ft deep.*

34

3 Cross the outlet and end of the lake to join a embanked path below where piped water from Llyn Melynllyn falls to be channeled into the lake, and continue on the path angling up the hillside on the line of the hidden pipeline, to eventually cross a small footbridge at the NE. corner of Llyn Melynllyn. From here, a track just out of sight, heads SE, to pass a ruined building.*The remains*

Penygadair

Pen·y·gaer

a clear path, initially above the river, soon rising to follow a wall up to cross the iron ladder-stile.

5 Cross the nearby footbridge, then follow a path contouring across the boulder-covered slope, later guided by occasional concrete posts, to cross an iron ladder-stile. The pathCrosses a stream, briefly runs alongside a wall, then follows a series of waymarker posts to another iron ladder-stile. Continue ahead. After a wall gap, the waymarked path goes half-LEFT up to go through another wall-gap and on to pass a ruined hafod. At the end of a walled section, the path rises LEFT and meanders across the hillside guided by waymarker posts to eventually reach a wall/fence corner. Follow the fence to a ladder-stile, where you rejoin your outward route.

② *Afon Ddu* ⑤

footbridge

Afon Melynllyn

N

0 ¼ mile

walk 21

④

of a wheelpit and old machinery are associated with the former Melynllyn slate quarry (1867-1908) on the slopes beyond. The track – the former tramway serving the quarry – continues across the mid-slopes, offering good views of your outward route. After a while it begins a long steady descent via two ladder-stiles, then levels out, before meandering down towards the adjoining expansive valley, with a good view of Llyn Eigiau. Just before a ladder-stile by a gate, turn sharp LEFT onto another track.

4 Follow the track down to cross a small dam over the Afon Melynllyn. Bear LEFT over the Afon Ddu to cross a ladder-stile (For **Walk C** follow a path heading half-left, rising steadily across open ground to join the main route at the footbridge) Continue ahead passing above the nearby building, then follow

Llyn Dulyn

ROWEN TO LLANBEDR-Y-CENNIN

DESCRIPTION A 6 mile walk on good paths, tracks and quiet lanes exploring the attractive undulating countryside between two attractive villages. The route works its way south to skirt the eastern slopes of Pen-y-Gaer, with an optional extension up to the Iron Age hillfort, before heading for Llanbedr-y-Cennin, with its old country inn. The return includes a section of delightful riverside walking. Allow about 3½ hours.

START Rowen [SH 761719].

DIRECTIONS Just after entering the village from the PO/stores, there is roadside parking on the right by the first houses.

1 Continue along the road into the village. At a stone memorial to Huw T.Edwards just before the Ty Gwyn Hotel, turn LEFT on a signposted path over the river. Go past Pen y Bont tearoom, through a gate and follow an old walled green track to an old farm. Go half-RIGHT past the end of the building and follow the enclosed path to cross an iron ladder-stile. Head across the field to cross another ladder-stile. Follow the green track up to a gateway. Ignore the ladder-stile, and turn RIGHT to follow the boundary on your left up to cross a ladder-stile in the top field corner. Follow the enclosed path down to cross a ladder-stile near a cottage. Turn RIGHT along the field edge. Go through a gateway and follow the waymarked path over two ladder-stiles, then turn LEFT up a track through the trees.

2 After going through a gate, follow the fence on your left above an old sunken track up the edge of three fields to cross an iron ladder-stile. Follow the next field edge, go through an old gateway and on to cross a ladder-stile. Follow a clear path ahead, later running alongside the remains of another old sunken track, to cross a ladder-stile by a small stone sheep-fold. Follow the enclosed path to a road. Follow it LEFT, then shortly turn RIGHT to pass between an outbuilding and the gated entrance to Waen Isa to cross a stone stile by a gate. Head half-LEFT up to go through a gate, and follow a path passing to the right of a large pylon. Go through a gap in an old wall and on across the large field past a telegraph post to cross a ladder-stile. Turn LEFT along the road, then RIGHT at a junction and continue up the lane.

3 On the bend take the signposted path on the left. (To visit Pen-y Gaer, continue up the lane for 50 yards to take a signposted path on the left to cross a fence. If no stile a gate a little higher provides access. Head half-right up the steep gorse-covered hillside to a wall and follow it up to a ladder-stile and a path leading to the fort.) Go through two gates past an old farm and along a faint green track. After about 75 yards, go half-RIGHT to follow a path, soon rising across the gorse-covered hillside then contouring across the slope to cross a ladder-stile in the nearby wall. Turn RIGHT along the path up to cross another ladder-stile. Follow the path across the slope, then go half-LEFT down to cross a ladder-stile. Head half-RIGHT through the bracken to walk beneath an embankment supporting a leat above. About 100 yards from the stile, as the leat embankment bends away, continue ahead to go through a gap in an old wall to follow a path through a bracken-covered field, soon angling gently down to cross a ladder-stile.

4 Turn LEFT to follow a delightful enclosed green track meandering steadily down the part-wooded hillside, passing through a gate to reach a junction of tracks by outbuildings. Turn RIGHT to follow the green track down to pass Cae Asaph, then swing LEFT past an outbuilding down its access track. Turn LEFT along a hedge-lined track, soon descending steeply to a lane by cottages. Follow it LEFT to a junction. Turn RIGHT down the road into Llanbedr-y-cennin to reach the junction by Ye Olde Bull Inn. *The village, which lies on a drovers route across the Carneddau mountains, is also known for Ffynnon Bedr, a holy well said to have cura-*

tive properties. Turn LEFT up the road past St. Peter's medieval church then a side road. Continue down the road. On the bend by Cennin Cottage go through the gate ahead to follow the signposted path along a track past Primose Bank Cottage to cross a ladder-stile.

5 Follow the boundary on your left down to cross a ladder-stile, and go down the next field edge to cross another ladder-stile on the right just before a house. Continue down near the garden wall to go through a gate and on past the end of a large outbuilding. Turn LEFT through a gateway below and go on to cross a ladder-stile by the river. Cross the farm's access lane and the stile opposite, and follow the stiled riverside path through three fields, before angling away from the river to follow the fence round a small wood and up to cross a ladder-stile in the top field corner. Turn RIGHT along the road over the river, and at a junction, turn LEFT. Continue along the road, soon crossing the river. Just before another bridge over the river, take a signposted path through a kissing gate on the left. Walk along the edge of the long and narrowing field by the river to cross a ladder-stile. Bear LEFT across the field to join your outward route at the old farm. Follow it back to Rowen, where its tearoom or country inn makes a refreshing finale!

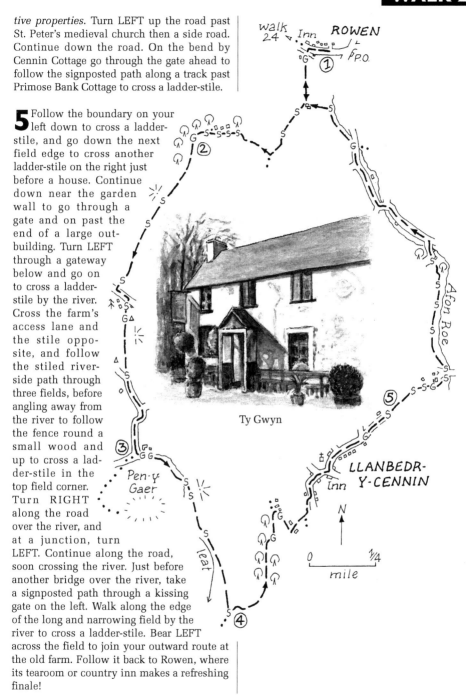

Ty Gwyn

walk 24

Inn ROWEN
P.O.
①

②

③ Pen-y-Gaer

④

⑤

LLANBEDR-Y-CENNIN
Inn

Afon Roe

N

0   ¼
mile

ST. CELYNIN'S CHURCH AND TAL Y FAN

DESCRIPTION A choice of routes exploring a fascinating scenic upland landscape, full of antiquity, featuring a remote ancient church, Maen Penddu and other standing stones, an ancient burial chamber, hillfort, a section of Roman road, combined with panoramic views. The main 7 mile walk (**A**) includes an exhilarating climb along the ridge of Taly y Fan, at just under 2000ft, Snowdonia's most northerly mountain. Although not a difficult ascent, this is for experienced walkers and should not be attempted in poor visibility. Allow about 5 hours. Lower level alternative 5½ mile (**B**) and 6½ mile (**C**) walks are included.
START Rowen [SH 761719].
DIRECTIONS Just after entering the village from the PO/stores, there is roadside parking on the right by the first houses.

I Walk through the village past the Ty Gwyn Hotel, attractive stone houses and a chapel. On the bend turn RIGHT on a signposted path along a lane to a farm. Go through the gate ahead and down the field to its left-hand corner and cross a ladder-stile ahead. Turn RIGHT along a track and on the bend cross a ladder-stile. Continue along the field edge, over another ladder-stile and follow the path up the field edge to a road. Turn RIGHT. Shortly, take a signposted path up a lane on the left to cross a ladder-stile at its end just before a farm. Follow the wall on your right, and at its corner, go half-RIGHT up to join a track and follow it behind the ruin. The track now angles up the part-wooded slope, crosses a small stream, before bending left then right. Continue up the track for a further 120 yards to a waymarked tree and cross a ladder-stile/stream to your right in the trees. Go half-LEFT up to a field and continue up alongside an old boulder wall, then head to a gate between an old cottage and outbuilding. Pass behind the cottage.

2 20 yards beyond, at a tree, turn sharp LEFT to follow a path angling up the slope, passing beneath gorse to follow a wall up to a ladder-stile. Go up the small grass ridge ahead, then across a reedy area, and along the left-hand side of another small ridge, with a ruin to your left. Continue up the field, with the church now visible, to cross a ladder-stile in the top corner. At a cross-track turn RIGHT to visit St Celynin's church. *St Celynin's church is a delightful simple building, whose nave dates from the 14thC. Summer services and harvest thanksgiving are still held here. In the south corner of the churchyard is a rectangular well, renowned for its power to heal sick children. Near the churchyard gate once stood an inn which served travellers crossing the mountains.* Return along the track and past a ladder-stile. Shortly, at a track junction, keep ahead to follow a green track up to a gate by sheepfolds. Keep ahead to follow the right fork of the track up across upland pasture.

3 About 200 yards before the wall ahead, where the path splits, you have a choice.

For **Walk B** take the left fork and continue up the green track curving round the western side of the hill. About half-way round, the track bears half-RIGHT, rising gently, then fades to a path after a stream, and continues alongside the wall ahead. After passing a small triangular enclosure, bear RIGHT – *the mound on your right is Caer Bach, a 1st millennium BC. hillfort* – and follow the wall, soon more ruinous, on your left up to go through a gate. Keep alongside the wall to cross two ladder-stiles, then follow the main path, later rejoining the wall to cross another ladder-stile. Follow the green track down to go through two gates below Cae Coch, then cross a ladder-stile onto a track at point **5**. Turn LEFT.

For **Walk A** take the right fork to cross a stream by the wall corner. Follow the path alongside the wall on your right, past the start of an alternative route to Maen Penddu via the right bank of the stream as shown. As the wall begins to descend, join a green track angling back on the left. It rises across

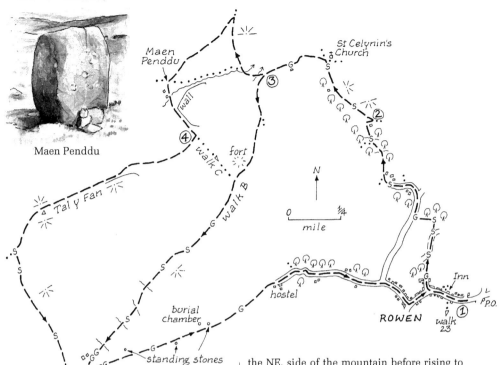

Maen Penddu

the gorse-covered pasture grazed by ponies towards Tal y Fan, to reach the large standing stone of Maen Penddu. *This flat-topped stone, almost 2 metres high, and an almost buried stone circle nearby, date from the 2nd millennium BC. and were of likely ceremonial importance.* Here, turn LEFT and follow a path to cross a stream by the second of two ruins. The path now rises to continue alongside a wall. As the wall begins to gently curve continue straight ahead on a path. After about 100 yards the ground begins to descend. (For **Walk C** continue ahead down the slope to join **Walk B** at the old wall near Cae Bach hillfort.)

4 For **Walk A**, head half-RIGHT across the boulder-covered slope to join a well-used path heading directly up the mountain, about 100 yards from a ruin to your left. At the top of the slope, the path briefly bears right, then continues across a depression on the NE. side of the mountain before rising to reach the wall on the Tal y Fan ridge. A good path following the wall along the ridge leads to the summit trig point, *with its breathtaking views.* Cross back over the ladder-stile and continue along the ridge, soon crossing a small gully, before beginning a long descent, to cross a ladder-stile visible some distance ahead. Now simply follow the clear, occasionally waymarked, stiled path down the southern slopes of Tal y Fan to a road. Turn LEFT and on the bend continue ahead along a track to the entrance to Cae Coch.

5 Now follow the old enclosed green lane, soon on a steady descent, to reach the Youth Hostel, then continue down the steep road into Rowen. *The lane is an ancient route, which later became part of the important Roman road from Canovium Roman fort in the Conwy valley to Segontium fort at Caernarfon. The adjoining slopes contain much evidence of early man. En route you pass Maen y Bard Neolithic burial chamber and 2nd millennium BC. standing stones.*

PRONUNCIATION

These basic points should help non-Welsh speakers

Welsh	English equivalent
c	always hard, as in cat
ch	as on the Scottish word loch
dd	as th in then
f	as in of
ff	as in off
g	always hard as in got
ll	no real equivalent. It is like 'th' in then, but with an 'L' sound added to it, giving 'thlan' for the pronunciation of the Welsh 'Llan'.

In Welsh the accent usually falls on the last-but-one syllable of a word.

KEY TO THE MAPS

- ━▶ Walk route and direction
- ═══ Metalled road
- ‾‾‾ Unsurfaced road
- •••• Footpath/route adjoining walk route
- ⌇⟶ River/stream
- ⚘☾ Trees
- ■■■ Railway
- **G** Gate
- **S** Stile
- ⟩⟨ Viewpoint
- Ⓟ Parking
- Ⓣ Telephone

THE COUNTRYSIDE CODE

- Be safe – plan ahead and follow any signs

- Leave gates and property as you find them

- Protect plants and animals, and take your litter home

- Keep dogs under close control

- Consider other people

This book is dedicated to Bluey, who was my constant companion during its writing, and is greatly missed.

The CroW Act 2000, implemented throughout Wales in May 2005, introduced new legal rights of access for walkers to designated open country, predominantly mountain, moor, heath or down, plus all registered common land. This access can be subject to restrictions and closure for land management or safety reasons for up to 28 days a year.

Published by
Kittiwake
3 Glantwymyn Village Workshops, Glantwymyn, Machynlleth, Montgomeryshire SY20 8LY

© Text & map research: David Berry 2006
© Maps & illustrations: Kittiwake 2006
Drawings by Morag Perrott
Cover photographs by David Berry.

I wish to thank Conwy County Borough Council Highways Department and Forest Enterprise for their invaluable advice and assistance.

Care has been taken to be accurate. However neither the author nor the publisher can accept responsibility for any errors which may appear, or their consequences. If you are in any doubt about access, check before you proceed.
Printed by MWL, Pontypool.

ISBN: **978 1 902302 56 0**

Printed by BoD™in Norderstedt, Germany